can it, bottle it, smoke it

KAREN SOLOMON
Photography by ANGIE CAO

can it, bottle it, smoke it

AND OTHER KITCHEN PROJECTS

TEN SPEED PRESS
Berkeley

Some of the recipes in this book include raw eggs, meat, or fish. When these foods are consumed raw, there is always the risk that bacteria, which is killed by proper cooking, may be present. For this reason, when serving these foods raw, always buy certified salmonella-free eggs and the freshest meat and fish available from a reliable grocer, storing them in the refrigerator until they are served. Because of the health risks associated with the consumption of bacteria that can be present in raw eggs, meat, and fish, these foods should not be consumed by infants, small children, pregnant women, the elderly, or any persons who may be immunocompromised.

Copyright © 2011 by Karen Solomon
Photographs copyright © 2011 by Angie Cao

All rights reserved.
Published in the United States by Ten Speed Press, an imprint of the Crown Publishing Group, a division of Random House, Inc., New York.
www.crownpublishing.com
www.tenspeed.com

Ten Speed Press and the Ten Speed Press colophon are registered trademarks of Random House, Inc.

Library of Congress Cataloging-in-Publication Data

Solomon, Karen.
  Can it, bottle it, smoke it : and other kitchen projects / Karen Solomon.
    p. cm.
  Includes index.
  Summary: "This innovative cookbook offers ideas for adventurous culinary DIYers to stock the pantry with artisan food and drink, kitchen staples, tasty snacks, and gift-worthy eats"—Provided by publisher.
  1. Canning and preserving. 2. Smoked food. 3. Food—Preservation. I. Title.
  TX603.S649 2011
  641.4—dc22
                                    2010045282

ISBN 978-1-58008-575-5

Printed in China

Design by Betsy Stromberg
Food styling by Karen Shinto
Prop styling by Daniele Kent Maxwell

10 9 8 7 6 5 4 3 2 1

First Edition

To Matthew, Emmett,
Desmond, and Mabel

contents

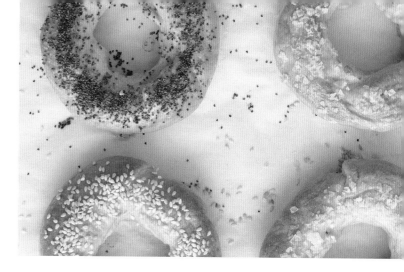

3 stock it

4 pickle it

5 bake it

6 stalk it

12 milk it

13 slurp it

14 freeze it

acknowledgments

If it takes a village to raise a child, it takes an idiot to write a cookbook. In this case, however, this idiot did not work alone. There are about a jillion people in my universe who deserve recognition and appreciation, and I'm likely going to forget many of them. But, if memory serves me correctly. . . .

My first laurel goes to Samantha Tackeff, my intern extraordinaire. She helped birth these recipes when they were just babies, and then did far more than her fair share of clean-up in their wake. And then there was all that testing, tasting, suggestions, and so on. Each and every one of you reading this should hire her at an extremely high salary to do something really, really excellent.

What you may not realize is that the only reason my food looks good is because of the world's best food stylist and recipe tester, Karen Shinto. And thank god a professional like Betsy Stromberg was in charge of the book's design/layout. You gals make food look good.

Clancy Drake is an editorial force to be reckoned with, and a genius in her field. I also thank my agent, Danielle Svetcov of Levine Greenberg, who is worth her weight in sugar and salt. Additionally, I thank Lisa Westmoreland, Ten Speed Press, and Random House for giving me another go.

Other folks to thank in no particular order: Anika Luskin Streitfeld for being the hub of the universe, Adam C. Boardman for the creative soundboarding and the additions to my vintage Tupperware stash, Celia Sack of Omnivore Books in San Francisco for research assistance, and all of my friends who were kind enough to eat all the "mistake food" that was part of the learning curve. Thanks to my fellow food obsessives in the blogosphere for your endless electron stream of kindness.

A huge shout-out to Josh Adler, formerly of food/art space 18Reasons, for the idea to do the Jam It Salon, my beloved quarterly gathering in San Francisco that forces us food crafters out of the kitchen and into a social setting, tastes in tow. And thanks to Rachel Cole and Rosie Branson Gill who continue to support the gathering. True heartfelt appreciation to everyone who has shown up at this event and shared your pickles, homebrew, preserves, baked goods, and wisdom. You are an inspiration to me every single time. In this same vein, I thank everyone who came to every bookstore appearance and shared their grandmother's recipes, their kitchen lore, and their love of food crafting and kitchen preservation of all stripes.

Food doesn't happen without music, right? Therefore I would be remiss if I did not shed some *gracias* on Lady Gaga, Arcade Fire, Missy Elliot, every incarnation of Stephin Merritt, the power of MOG, and whoever else made my kitchen sing.

Thank you to Joyce Slaton Lollar for the world's best punk rock Hello Kitty skull apron; I will always treasure it and wear it to every event. Thank you to my family for your continued support—and for putting up with all that take-out food even though, by all appearances, I had been in the kitchen all day (note: this is every food writer's secret shame). Thank you, food eaters everywhere, for your support.

introduction

Call it punk domesticity, urban domestics, hipsters with Mason jars, or just a CAN-do attitude: a humongous tidal swell of interest in food preservation, home canning, foraging, nose-to-tail eating, and back-to-basics DIY kitchen wizardry has been growing in the past few years, and the movement has permanently shaped the way we think about store-bought and packaged foods of all sorts. Obsessive food eaters like you and me are demanding in earnest the same high-quality, artisanal standards from factory-prepared foods like cereals and sodas that we've sought out in our organic produce, hormone-free dairy, and grass-fed beef. In short, we've grown hungry as hell for real food, and we see no need to stomach mass market cookie-cutter food any longer.

Home cooks have burned our palates on too much overbulked food packed with guar gum, dyes, and stabilizers. We've grown weary of characterless crackers, condiments, cereals, and other same-same packaged food solutions that continue to dominate the interior aisles of the grocery store. Who wants uniform factory-fake food that always tastes the same and looks the same?

We've come to expect more from what we eat, and we're happy to inject a little sweat equity in our food—donning an apron, picking up a wooden spoon, and forging our own path to good eating and kitchen fun.

Making your own food is awesome. And, in point of pride, crafting your own pantry staples outshines the assembling of a single meal any day. Make chicken and rice and you can eat tonight. Make catsup and miso and you can enjoy the fruits of your labor for months.

When I wrote *Jam It, Pickle It, Cure It,* my first book on DIY cooking projects, I spent a year in the kitchen tinkering and experimenting to find the best and shortest routes to the kinds of handmade cooking projects that felt, at least to me, overlooked—lard, mustard, and marshmallows among them. My goals were simple: make a wide swath of the best project-y eats, using the least amount of effort and specialty gear, in my own urban apartment kitchen. I loved this notion of putting my own stamp on larder staples. I enjoyed writing *Jam It* so much, but I felt limited by a short production time, and I always felt just a few recipes short of finishing the kitchen manual that I'd always longed to own.

Each recipe was like a stand-mixer-windstorm that blew open a dozen new pages of ideas for additional projects. Making frozen fruit pops made me want to try out alcohol-infused pops. Infusing oil naturally got me thinking about full-flavored vinegars. Making sausage steered my thoughts to the possibility of homemade hot dogs and, of course, to handcrafting the ever-present and necessary elongated bun. Was it possible to do all this at home adhering to these same principles? The only way to know for sure was to give it a go.

And once I started talking to other food-crafting enthusiasts in bookstores and online, I immediately started acquiring new material: family fixes and recipes and a grandmother's archive of pantry staple ideas. One woman told me of her grandmother's pickles fermented with a slice of rye bread floating on top. Another gave me her recipe for plum brandy, made with nothing but garden plums, sugar, and plenty of time. And I'd never had so many conversations about raising chickens in my backyard! I am thankful to everyone who shared with me all of those great kitchen ideas.

I'm also thankful to all of you kooky cooks and bloggers who gave *Jam It* a try, and I sincerely hope that it led to some brainstorming at your own kitchen counter—that you, too, realized that you can do it better than the faceless food factory. I'm also thankful to Ten Speed Press for continuing to take a gamble on the culinary trials, errors, and successes of one dedicated, hard-working, heavy-researching food geek.

Yes, you CAN can. And dry. And ferment. And bottle. And bake. AND SMOKE. This book will give you a few more ways to do it all to the best of your ability. Enjoy, happy crafting, and keep pushing your food lust to the limits of kitchen science and your own palate's creative genius.

Karen Solomon
CanItBottleItSmokeIt.com

1 | jam it

In the oeuvre of jam-making, we have the classics: strawberry, blueberry, grape, marmalade, and so on. And while these blue-chip jams are always crowd-pleasers, one should never get stuck in a fruity rut, but instead venture forth into new ingredients and new flavor combinations destined to become your new favorite spreads on bread.

Head into the kitchen with your head held high. Cut your culinary chops on a carrot almond jam, stir up a classic apricot jam, channel your inner Spaniard with quince paste, and start dunking the entire contents of your refrigerator into addictive plum catsup. And the firm, sliceable fruit cheese here will also keep your dairy bin in action.

Remember that good jam starts with good fruit: never use overripe fruit or anything not perfect enough to eat out of hand. March to the farmers' market and scope out what's good right now. Your jam pot awaits.

carrot almond jam

Makes about 4 cups
(2 pints)

TIME COMMITMENT
About 2 hours

This jam is an extension of a failed recipe for Passover carrot candy from an ancient cookbook put out by a home for the aged in Worcester, Massachusetts. I've abandoned ship on making the candy, but this jam is an unusual and sweet treat unto itself. I also dig this one because all of the produce isn't super seasonally dependent. Not only will this add veggie power to your breakfast toast, but it's fah-bu-lous mixed with cream cheese as a frosting for carrot cake. If you can't find tamari almonds, just roasted and salted ones will work.

1 1/2 pounds carrots, trimmed, peeled, and shredded (about 4 1/4 cups)

1 teaspoon grated fresh ginger

2 1/2 cups sugar

1/2 cup water

1/2 cup chopped tamari almonds

1 thin-skinned orange

1 lemon

INSTRUCTIONS Combine the carrots, ginger, sugar, and water in a large Dutch oven. In a food processor, grind the nuts and add them to the pot. Wash the orange and lemon and cut them into quarters. Chop them—seeds, skins, and all—in the food processor, and then stir them into the pot as well.

Put the pot over medium heat, cover, and let it come to a boil. Stir, turn the heat to medium-low, cover again, and let simmer for 40 minutes, stirring occasionally, allowing the carrots to get tender.

HOW TO STORE IT Spoon the jam into clean jars and refrigerate for up to 3 months. Or spoon into sterilized canning jars, packing very tightly to eliminate the air bubbles inside (you can also stick a chopstick or long skewer into the jar to pop the bubbles before canning). Process for 15 minutes (review the canning instructions on page 28). This will keep for up to 1 year on the shelf.

apricot orange jam

Makes about 7 cups
(3 1/2 pints)

TIME COMMITMENT
about 1 1/2 hours

A little citrus can go a long way in jam-making—it both brightens sweet fruit flavors and helps thicken fruit-and-sugar mixtures. This lovely summer jam is not overly sweet, and it shows off the apricots' best attributes. Use thick-skinned oranges like navels or Valencias.

2 1/2 pounds apricots, pitted and sliced lengthwise
1 cup minced orange peel (from about 2 large oranges)
4 cups sugar
Juice of one lemon
3 cups Apple Pectin (page 12)

INSTRUCTIONS Place a small plate in the freezer.

Combine the apricots, orange peel, sugar, and lemon juice in a large Dutch oven and let macerate for at least 1 hour to extract the juice from the fruit.

Cover the pot and bring the fruit mixture to a rapid boil over medium-high heat. Remove the cover and stir often for 5 minutes, to keep the temperature even and keep the fruit from sticking to the bottom. Turn off the heat and, once the bubbling has stopped, stir in the pectin to combine. Test a teaspoonful of the jam on the chilled plate. After 30 seconds, the jam should be viscous and streak slowly when the plate is tilted.

HOW TO STORE IT Pour the jam into clean glass jars and refrigerate for up to 4 months. Or pour it into sterile canning jars and process for 15 minutes (review the canning instructions on page 28). This will keep for up to 1 year on the shelf.

quince paste

Makes about 6 ounces

TIME COMMITMENT
about 1 1/2 hours

Quince are fall and winter fruit and they're very high in pectin, making them a dream for jams and jellies. This preparation is called a paste, but it's really sort of an adult fruit chew just born to sit alongside Manchego cheese and Marcona almonds. Don't let the week-long preparation time deter you; most of that is just curing time.

3/4 pound quince, peeled, cored, and cut into 1-inch cubes
2/3 cup sugar
2/3 cup water
1/4 teaspoon kosher salt
1/4 cup fresh lemon juice (from about 2 lemons)

INSTRUCTIONS Line a small rectangular baking dish (about 6 by 4 inches) with parchment paper, and lightly oil the paper with a neutral vegetable oil.

Combine the quince, sugar, water, and salt in a medium saucepan. Cover, and bring to a boil over medium-high heat. Reduce heat to a simmer and stir occasionally for 20 to 25 minutes, until the fruit completely breaks down and the mixture turns a dark, caramel color. Draw a spoon across the bottom of the pot; the mixture should streak and hold its shape before flowing together again. Mash the mixture with the back of a spoon or with a potato masher (or carefully spoon it into a food processor and puree it for a totally smooth consistency). Stir in the lemon juice. Pour the hot paste into the paper-lined dish and let it set at room temperature for 4 days. Lift the paste out of the dish with the paper and invert onto a flat surface covered with oil-lined parchment paper; let it cure for an additional 3 days at room temperature, uncovered. The dried and cured paste should be firm throughout and slightly tacky on the outside.

Using a knife or a bench scraper, trim the edges of the paste to make them even and attractive (that is, if you like your food even and attractive).

HOW TO STORE IT Wrap the paste tightly in wax paper and store in the refrigerator for up to 1 year.

plum catsup

Makes about 4 cups

TIME COMMITMENT
about 1 1/2 hours

Where does one draw the line between a catsup and a sauce? My personal definition is that if I want to dunk French fries in it, it's a catsup. This hot little number is way more versatile than your standard bottled tomato catsup. It's tangy, sweet, severely savory—killer on a chicken sandwich or with pork loin. Find a friend with a plum tree (thanks, Tom!) and you will have plums a-plenty to get this in gear.

5 pounds black or red plums, preferably Santa Rosas

2 cups water

1 1/3 cups sugar

2/3 cup plus 2 tablespoons apple cider vinegar

6 tablespoons orange marmalade

1 large cinnamon stick

2 star anise

2 whole cloves garlic, peeled and lightly scored with the tip of a knife

4 teaspoons kosher salt

INSTRUCTIONS Wash and stem the plums and lay them in a single layer in the bottom of a large Dutch oven. Add the water. Cover and bring to a boil over high heat. Reduce the heat and simmer for 30 minutes, stirring occasionally to prevent the fruit from sticking to the pot. The skins will burst and the plums will release their juice and soften.

Remove the pot from the heat, uncover it, and let the fruit cool for about 5 minutes. Pour the plums into a heavy-duty sieve, a small-holed colander, or a food mill set over a large mixing bowl and push the plums through to render the juice and the pulp and to separate out the skins and the pits. Discard the skins and pits. Return the juice and the pulp to the pot and add the sugar, vinegar, marmalade, cinnamon, star anise, garlic, and salt.

Set the pot over high heat and bring it just to a boil. Lower the heat and simmer the mixture, uncovered, to reduce it, being careful not to let it splatter. Stir often, modifying the heat as needed to keep it at a slow simmer as the liquid reduces. Cook for about 35 minutes, until the mixture has thickened. Draw a spoon across the bottom of the pot; the mixture should be thick enough to part, expose the bottom of the pot, and then come back together again. Remove and discard the cinnamon, anise, and garlic. Pour the catsup into glass jars or bottles.

HOW TO STORE IT Kept refrigerated, this catsup will keep for up to 1 year. It can be served warm or cold.

apple cranberry fruit cheese

Makes about 11 ounces

TIME COMMITMENT
2 to 3 days

Where does a fruit paste begin and a fruit cheese end? On the culinary map, I believe it's somewhere around the intersection of Yum and Awesome. Fruit cheese tastes like fruit but slices like cheese, and it comes complete with a surprisingly creamy texture. It's beautiful, and in addition to tasting swell on its own, it turns any humble plate of Cheddar cheese and crackers into a rather swanky hors d'oeuvre.

1½ pounds sweet apples, peeled, cored, and cut into 1-inch cubes (about 4 cups)

⅓ cup dried cranberries

½ cup water

¾ cup sugar

¼ teaspoon kosher salt

INSTRUCTIONS Combine all the ingredients in a large saucepan, cover, and bring to a boil over high heat. Reduce the heat and simmer for 20 to 25 minutes, until the fruit is very tender. Reduce the heat to low, uncover, and mash with the back of a spoon or a potato masher. Allow the fruit to thicken and slowly reduce for about 1 hour, until the mixture darkens, mashing and stirring frequently to keep it from burning or sticking. The mixture will be thick enough to part and expose the bottom of the pot before slowly coming together again.

While the fruit is cooking, line a loaf pan with a sheet of parchment paper long enough that an inch or two hangs over each long side. Lightly oil the paper with vegetable oil and pour the fruit mixture into the lined pan, smoothing it out evenly with a spoon or spatula. It will be about ⅜ inch thick. Refrigerate, uncovered, for 24 hours.

Take the fruit cheese out of the refrigerator. Grasping the paper, lift it from the pan and transfer it to a rack on top of a baking sheet. The cheese should retain its shape. If it doesn't, return it to the pan and refrigerate for another day before moving forward.

Turn on the oven to its lowest setting and place the fruit cheese—paper, rack, and all—in the oven. Dry the fruit cheese in the oven for 3 hours, with a wooden spoon propping open the oven door to let moisture escape. The cheese should feel dry on top when it's done. If it's not, return it to the oven for another hour. Allow the fruit cheese to sit at room temperature for 1 day. The next day, lay a clean piece of parchment paper on the rack and invert the cheese onto the new paper, so that its bottom side is facing up. Put the cheese—rack, paper, and all—back into a low oven for 3 hours. The cheese has cured when the surface feels dry to the touch (but don't worry if it's still quite moist in the middle).

HOW TO STORE IT Once it's cooled completely, wrap the cheese tightly in wax paper and store it in the dairy drawer of the refrigerator. It will keep (and, in fact, improve), when stored well-wrapped, for 6 months.

apple pectin

Makes about 2 1/2 cups

TIME COMMITMENT
7 to 12 hours

Back in the day, there was no Sure-Jell. If you wanted your berry jam to thicken up when the fruit was bursting off the vines in August, you turned to the green apples that were planning to sweeten up in the fall. Homemade pectin is not as strong or as dependable as the stuff in the package, but I am in love with the idea of making my cooking projects as humanly as possible. I will always be happier with a slightly runny toast spread than one that is so artificially stiff it can barely move. Dare I say it's the jam-maker's equivalent of the difference between silicone implants and the feel of real? Note that you can use red apples for pectin, but your finished product will have a pinkish hue. This is okay if you're going to use the pectin later in strawberry jam, but you might not want it in peaches. Pectin-making is also a great use for all the skins and cores that stem from making your own applesauce or apple butter.

5 pounds green apples or crab apples, preferably underripe
3 cups water

INSTRUCTIONS Wash and stem the apples, cutting away any bruising. If the apples are small, leave them whole. If they are large, cut them into halves or quarters, keeping the skins and cores intact (this is where most of the pectin in the fruit resides).

Place the fruit in a large stockpot or Dutch oven and add the water. Cover, bring to a boil over high heat, then reduce to a simmer for at least 45 minutes, stirring occasionally, until the apples turn to total mush.

Line a colander with a clean cotton cloth, and place the colander over a large, very clean bucket or bowl. Pour the apple mixture into the cloth and let the liquid drain into the bowl beneath. This liquid is your pectin. Do not press on the apples, or else the pectin (and later your jam) will turn cloudy. Allow the liquid to drain for at least 6 hours or overnight, stirring the mash occasionally.

Once the liquid stops dripping completely even after stirring, discard the solids. Test the pectin for effectiveness. In a small bowl, combine 2 tablespoons rubbing alcohol with 1 tablespoon of the pectin and stir with a fork. Wait for gelatinous solid material to form that is solid enough to be picked up with a fork. If the pectin is still a bit stringy and not solid, pour the pectin into a small saucepan, place over high heat, reduce it to a simmer and let it reduce, uncovered, until it is reduced by half, about 15 minutes. Let cool completely and test the pectin again.

HOW TO STORE IT To store the pectin, keep it in the refrigerator for up to 1 week, or freeze airtight for several months. You may also can pectin as you would jam, pouring it into sterilized canning jars, processing it in boiling water for 15 minutes, and keeping it on the shelf for up to 1 year. (Review the canning instructions on page 28.)

To use pectin in jams or jellies, use equal amounts of pectin and fresh cut-up fruit. For example, 2 cups of fruit will require 2 cups of pectin.

2 | spoon it

Breakfast. For some, it is merely the first meal of the day. For me, it's the thing I dream about as I'm going to sleep at night. I am a serious cereal junkie. For as long as I can remember, I have had a sort of obsessive-compulsive disorder that requires me to have at least seven open boxes of cereal at any one time. On lazy weekend mornings, however, I have found myself wondering what it would be like to pour my morning bowl from something other than a store-bought box. The results of my investigations follow.

Some of these, like the nuggets and the granolas, are giving trees: make them now and enjoy them for weeks to come. Others, such as the crispy rice and the cornflakes, are more fleeting, but still entirely worth the effort.

And giftable? You know it: all it takes is a jar, a tin, a clear bag tied with twine, and labels of your own creation. Or for those who lean toward over-achievement, your own face and design on a repurposed box.

Dig in, cerealholics. Let's spoon it.

cornflakes

Makes about 9 ounces

TIME COMMITMENT
about 15 minutes

There come moments in kitchen projectry when one has to ask oneself, "Is this insane? Have I crossed the line from food-craftiness into utter madness, making my own corn-flakes?" Search inside your gut and you will find the answer to that question for yourself. Should you decide to move forward, the recipe to fuel your fire is below. Now, if you need me, I'll be sitting in the corner over there, whittling my own toothpicks. . . .

2/3 cup corn flour or finely ground cornmeal
2 teaspoons kosher salt
1/4 cup sugar
11 ounces water

INSTRUCTIONS Preheat the oven to 350°F and oil two large rimmed baking sheets.

Combine the flour, salt, sugar, and water in a bowl and stir with a fork until smooth. Divide the batter evenly between the prepared pans. Tilt the pans to distribute the batter evenly over the entire surface of the pan. If needed, use a bowl scraper or spatula to help with this task.

Bake until the edges are brown and the cereal starts to pull away from the sides of the pan, 11 to 13 minutes.

Let the pans sit for about 30 seconds after you remove them from the oven. Use a spatula to lift up the cereal sheets and break them into bite-size flakes in the pan. Eat immediately.

HOW TO STORE IT Stored absolutely airtight (and refrigerated in humid weather), these will last for 3 days.

puffed rice

Makes about 3 1/2 cups

TIME COMMITMENT
about 7 hours

Sometimes magic happens right in our very own woks. This kind of puffed, crunchy rice is usually the stuff of savory Asian dishes—think sizzling rice soup. However, it is also a totally fun thing to spoon from a bowl with milk before noon—and the best at-home solution to puffed rice cereal (not to mention a great use for leftover rice). As a snack, it also pairs nicely with the crunchy lentils on page 106. The only drawback is that the crunch fades fast. You'd be wise to eat it right away, and stored airtight, it's really only at its best within a day. Any kind of nonsticky rice can be used here. However, note that it must be completely dry.

2 cups cooked long-grain rice
2 cups vegetable oil
4 teaspoons light brown sugar
1/4 teaspoon kosher salt
1/4 teaspoon ground cinnamon

INSTRUCTIONS Allow the rice to sit uncovered and at room temperature for at least 6 hours (or overnight) to dry out completely. Stir it occasionally and break up any clumps so that each grain is separate.

Place a wok over high heat for 3 minutes. Line a work surface or rimmed baking sheet with clean newspaper or paper towels. Pour the oil into the pan and allow it to get smoking hot (this will take about 5 minutes). Have a mesh skimmer at the ready to scoop the rice out of the pan.

Measure 1/3 cup of the rice and gently slide it into the hot oil. Stir immediately and keep stirring for 30 seconds; the rice will puff and get crispy. Working quickly, remove the rice with the skimmer, shaking it briefly above the wok to drain excess oil, and let it drain and cool in a single layer on the paper towels. Cook, drain, and cool the remaining rice in batches.

Once it's cooled, transfer the rice to a small mixing bowl and sprinkle with the sugar, salt, and cinnamon, tossing gently to coat evenly.

The rice is ready to eat immediately.

HOW TO STORE IT Stored airtight, it will last 1 day at most.

insanely healthy nuggets

Makes about 2 1/2 cups

TIME COMMITMENT
about 3 hours

This is a great gifting cereal—sturdy, attractive, packed with toothsome texture and morning flavors, and, shall we say, "motivating." Double baking gives these nuggets a solid bite. By all means, pour on the milk, but this is a good one to try with yogurt and fresh fruit, too. Note that a food processor is required for this recipe.

1 1/2 cups quick-cooking rolled oats

1 cup orange juice

3/4 cup apple juice

1/2 cup dried currants or raisins

1/2 teaspoon kosher salt

1/4 cup light brown sugar

2 tablespoons wheat germ

2 tablespoons flax seeds

1/2 cup sunflower seeds

1/4 cup chopped dates

1/4 cup shredded unsweetened coconut

1/2 cup whole hazelnuts

INSTRUCTIONS In a large mixing bowl, combine the oats with the orange juice and apple juice, making sure the oats are completely covered with juice, and let soak until the oats are very soft, about 30 minutes.

While the oats are soaking, preheat the oven to 375°F and line a large rimmed baking sheet with parchment paper.

Drain the oats, reserving the juice, and return the oats to the large bowl. Put the reserved juice in a small bowl, add the currants, and soak for about 15 minutes while you prepare the rest of the cereal.

Stir the oats vigorously with a fork until they break down and become a thick batter. Add the salt, sugar, wheat germ, flax seeds, sunflower seeds, dates, coconut, and hazelnuts.

Drain the currants (discarding the liquid this time) and add those to the mix, too. Stir to combine well.

Scrape the thick cereal batter into the prepared pan and press it into an even rectangular slab thin enough so that you can see the tops of the hazelnuts peeking out. Bake for 20 minutes, until the batter is set, dry to the touch, and starting to brown at the bottom.

Remove the pan from the oven and let the cereal cool in the pan until cool enough to handle. Meanwhile, preheat the oven again, this time to 200°F. Remove the parchment paper from the baking sheet and discard.

Break the sheet of cereal up into thirds with your hands. Place about 1/3 of the cooled cereal into a food processor fitted with the metal blade and give it 20 to 25 pulses, until the cereal is broken into pieces slightly smaller than peas. Transfer the chopped cereal into another vessel and pulse the remainder of the cereal in two more batches.

Spread the cereal on the baking sheet in a single, even layer. Place in the oven and let dry for 30 minutes. Remove the pan from the oven, stir the cereal, spread it out again, and return to the oven to dry for another 30 minutes.

The cereal is now ready to eat.

HOW TO STORE IT Allow it to cool completely in the pan before transferring to an airtight container. It will keep for at least 3 months in the refrigerator.

sesame rosemary granola

Makes about 6 cups

TIME COMMITMENT
about 45 minutes

This cereal has a lot going for it: mainly herbaceous nuttiness and crunch. Toasting the nuts and oats individually before the granola goes in the oven makes the final product exceedingly crunchy, and it's really not a ton of extra effort. Oh, and if apricots and cranberries aren't your thing, feel free to swap them out for your preferred dried fruit— enough to measure one cup.

1/3 cup white sesame seeds

1/2 cup chopped walnut pieces

1/2 cup whole cashews

3/4 cup unsweetened flaked coconut

3 cups quick-cooking rolled oats

1/3 cup flax seeds

1/3 cup plus 2 tablespoons dark brown sugar

1/3 cup plus 2 tablespoons neutral vegetable oil

1 teaspoon dried rosemary, minced fine

10 dried apricot halves, chopped into slivers (about 2/3 cup)

1/3 cup dried cranberries

INSTRUCTIONS Preheat the oven to 325°F.

Place a dry nonstick skillet over medium-high heat for 5 minutes. In the hot pan, toast the sesame seeds, walnuts, and cashews for 3 minutes, stirring often, until the sesame seeds pop and the nuts and seeds all turn light brown. Transfer to a mixing bowl. Then toast the coconut for

2 minutes, stirring frequently, until it begins to turn golden, and add it to the bowl. Add the oats to the pan and stir often for about 3 minutes, until they toast and brown. Transfer them to the bowl.

Add the flax seeds to the bowl and stir the nuts, seeds, and oats to mix well. Add the sugar, oil, and rosemary. Stir well to coat. Spread the mixture evenly on a large rimmed baking sheet. Bake for 15 minutes, stirring every 5 minutes to ensure even toasting.

Remove the cereal from the oven, transfer it to a bowl, and stir in the apricots and the cranberries.

The cereal can be eaten warm or cold.

HOW TO STORE IT For storage, let it cool completely (this will take about 1 hour). Transfer it to sealed jars or other airtight containers, and it will keep refrigerated for up to 6 months.

apple–candied fennel seed granola

Makes about 6 cups

TIME COMMITMENT
about 1 1/2 hours

I'm a big fan of black licorice and fennel flavors, and not only are those present in this mix courtesy of the candied fennel seed, but the brightly colored candy shells give this cereal a nice, vibrant, wake-you-up look. If you don't have an Indian grocer nearby, you can find these colorful lovelies online at IShopIndian.com. However, if you don't love the taste of Good & Plenty, licorice allsorts, or Icelandic licorice candy, by all means replace the candied fennel seed with raisins (or your other favorite dried fruit, or toasted nuts, or— what the heck—M&M's). I highly recommend making your own dried apples, as they are fresh and flavorful and not a ton of extra effort, but, of course, you can find them in a bag. To make your own, see the recipe on page 22.

3 cups quick-cooking rolled oats
1/2 cup neutral vegetable oil
1 cup chopped dried apples (see page 22)
1/3 cup candied fennel seed
1/2 teaspoon kosher salt
Pinch of black pepper
2/3 cup honey

INSTRUCTIONS Preheat the oven to 325°F.

In a cold cast-iron skillet over medium heat, combine the oats with 3 tablespoons of the vegetable oil, stir to coat the oats thoroughly with oil, and toast until fragrant and dry, about 20 minutes, stirring occasionally. (If you don't have a cast-iron skillet, any heavy skillet will do.)

Once the oats are toasted, add the remaining oil, the apple, fennel seed, salt, pepper, and honey to the pan and stir well to combine.

If you're not using a cast-iron or other oven-safe skillet, transfer the mixture to a baking sheet. Put the skillet or baking sheet in the oven and bake for 30 minutes, stirring and scraping from the bottom every 10 minutes.

The granola will form small clumps and brown as it bakes. It's delicious with milk right out of the oven.

HOW TO STORE IT For long-term storage, allow it to cool for at least 1 hour, stirring occasionally to keep it from sticking to the pan. Transfer to an airtight container and store in the refrigerator for up to 6 months.

// CONTINUED

PLUS: dried apples

Makes about 1 1/4 ounces

TIME COMMITMENT 2 to 3 hours

They're yummy in cereal, but dried apples also make a great snack on their own—particularly if you close your eyes and tell yourself you're eating fried chips. Imaginative leaps notwithstanding, these are an excellent use for an apple bounty and super easy to put together.

2 sweet apples

INSTRUCTIONS Preheat the oven to its lowest temperature setting. Wash and dry the apples and cut them into 1/8-inch slices using a sharp knife or a mandoline. There's no need to skin them, but do discard the cores. Lightly oil two wire racks and place each over a baking sheet. Arrange the apples on the racks in a single layer, and put the baking sheets in the oven, keeping the door ajar with a wooden spoon. Let the apples dry for 2 to 3 hours, checking on them after 2 hours. When finished, the fruit will be dry throughout and the edges will be curled and beginning to brown.

HOW TO STORE IT Let cool completely on the racks, and store in an airtight container in the refrigerator for up to 3 months.

energy balls!

Makes 18 power-pumped
balls

TIME COMMITMENT
about 1 1/2 hours

Ready? Set? HIPPIE SNACKS! If you want to take your cereal calories with you—sans milk—this is your recipe. And why the exclamation point? Because these brown orbs are calorically dense enough to ready you for a marathon, danceathon, or sportathon of choice. This works great with the Sesame Rosemary Granola on page 19, but any granola will do.

1/2 cup peanut butter

2 tablespoons honey

1/4 cup maple syrup

1/4 cup water

3 cups granola, homemade (page 19) or store-bought

1 tablespoon flax seeds

INSTRUCTIONS Preheat the oven to 425°F, and lightly oil a small baking sheet.

Combine all the ingredients in a bowl and mix well with a fork; the mixture will be stiff and sticky. With wet hands, roll the dough into 1 1/2-inch balls. Place them on the baking sheet, flattening them slightly as you do so.

Bake for 10 minutes; the tops of the balls will be light brown, but don't allow the bottoms to get too dark. Let cool on the pan for 1 hour.

HOW TO STORE IT Store in an airtight container, refrigerated, for up to 1 month.

3 | stock it

Oh brother, Mother Hubbard, have you checked out your cupboard? Look at all those crazy cans and bottles. Where did they come from? Who made them? How long did they travel to get here? And what's really lurking under the lids?

You can save yourself from the exotic stabilizers and questionable chemical additives in commercial pantry staples—and, sometimes, from spending more money than you need to.

Crafting your own DIY kitchen means that a little investment of time and energy now provides a pantry with your personal stamp for months to come. You may not reach for your homemade condiments and flavor enhancers every day, but when you do, you'll beam with pride. Make them, bottle them, share them—and stir in their sweet sweat equity.

canned tomatoes

Makes about 16 cups
(8 pints)

TIME COMMITMENT
about 4 hours

Think about it: how many dishes do you eat on a regular basis that begin with a can of tomatoes? I blaze through cases of the stuff in pasta sauces, braised meats, and vegetable soups alone. Canned tomatoes are the little black dress of the kitchen. They're always appropriate and entirely versatile, and they never go out of style. Why not make your canned tomatoes the very best that they can be, featuring plump red orbs from your favorite farmer packed at the height of the season? Cook's notes: Meyer lemons will not be acidic enough to properly preserve the fruit. Use any other kind of lemon juice. And be sure to use clean, crack-free jars and fresh canning lids (the bands can be previously used).

6½ pounds perfectly ripe tomatoes
8 teaspoons kosher salt
8 teaspoons lemon juice (from about 2 lemons)

INSTRUCTIONS Wash, stem, and core the tomatoes. Chop into ½-inch pieces, trying to retain as much of the juice as possible; I use a bench scraper to scoop up the juice and seeds and add them to the bowl that's holding my chopped tomatoes. You should have about 18 cups of fruit.

Tightly pack a little more than 2 cups of tomatoes into each of 8 clean pint jars with fresh lids ready for canning. Don't worry if the jars appear not to have enough headspace, as the tomatoes will reduce when they are processed. Make certain that the fruit is packed as firmly as possible without bruising it. Divide the tomato juices evenly among the jars. Sprinkle 1 teaspoon of salt and 1 teaspoon of lemon juice into each jar.

Examine the level of liquid of each jar, and top off with tap water as needed to fully cover the fruit. Cap each jar tightly and shake gently to distribute the salt and lemon juice.

HOW TO STORE IT Process according to the canning directions in the sidebar on page 28. Label and date the jars and store in a dark, cool place. Properly sealed, these cans will have a shelf life of 1 year.

HOW TO CAN IT

Place an empty canning pot or stockpot on the stovetop (don't turn on the heat yet). Place as many jars in the pot as will fit without touching one another (you may have to process the jars in multiple batches). Fill the pot with cold water to cover the jars by at least 1 inch. Put the lid on the pot and turn the heat to high. Bring the water to a boil and let the jars boil for 15 minutes.

Put a kitchen towel on your counter. Turn the heat off and carefully remove the jars from the hot water bath with tongs or canning tongs and place them on the towel (don't let the jars touch). You will likely hear some of the jar lids pop, indicating that they have been properly sealed (they can still be properly sealed even if you don't hear the pop). After the jars have cooled for about 10 minutes, check the seals: press down on the center of each lid; it should not bounce back. If it does, move the jar to the refrigerator once it's cool and eat within a week.

preserved lemons

Makes 4 cups

TIME COMMITMENT
about 1 week

Go out right now and make friends with people who have a lemon tree. Be nice to them. Bring them cookies from time to time and occasionally walk their dog. Do whatever it takes to encourage them to let you help yourself to their citrus bounty when the time comes. The rind of a preserved lemon may not be something we reach for every day, but no Moroccan tagine would be complete without its acidic tang (and, for something completely different, try a splash of the juice in your next Bloody Mary). Many commercial varieties preserve the fruit in citric acid. However, this homemade version is quick to put together and relies on only lemon juice and salt as preservatives, with great unique flavor that will last from one North African feast to the next. Cook's note: Meyer lemons should not be used for this recipe, as their skins are too thin.

4 pounds thick-skinned lemons

6 cloves

3 bay leaves

1 (4-inch) cinnamon stick

1/4 cup kosher salt

INSTRUCTIONS Wash, dry, and stem the 6 smallest lemons in the bunch (or however many whole lemons you can comfortably fit inside a quart jar). Take the lemons out of the jar and cut a deep X shape lengthwise into each fruit, leaving about 3/4 inch of each lemon intact at one end.

Place the cloves, bay, and cinnamon in the bottom of the jar. Pour all of the salt onto a plate. Hold a cut lemon over the plate and spoon 1 teaspoon of salt inside the cut.

Rub the salt all over the inside of the fruit and stack it in the jar. When all the lemons are packed in, scrape up any remaining salt and transfer that to the jar as well.

Juice the remaining lemons until you have 2 cups of juice—enough to cover all of the lemons in the jar. If you run out of lemon juice, pour in a small amount of water to top off the fruit. It's important that the lemons be totally submerged.

Cover the jar tightly, and shake gently to distribute the salt. Label and date the jar, and refrigerate for 7 days, shaking occasionally.

HOW TO STORE IT Your lemons are ready to use after a week and they will keep for up to 1 year in the refrigerator.

vanilla extract

Makes 1 cup

TIME COMMITMENT
about 8 weeks

When you make your own vanilla extract, the waiting time is long, but the labor involved is minimal. Essentially, you're supersaturating booze with real vanilla to make the most potent vanilla tincture you can imagine. Although I'm calling for vodka here because it's the most neutral in flavor, feel free to go wild with rum, whisky, amaretto, you name it: but if you do, expect that your extract will carry those flavors into whatever you're baking or flavoring. Vanilla beans are fairly expensive; I buy mine at Saffron.com, where the quality is high and the price astonishingly low.

8 vanilla beans
1 cup vodka

INSTRUCTIONS Using a sharp paring knife, split the vanilla beans along their length, keeping a half-inch of the bean intact at the stem end so you have something to hold onto while scraping. With your knife tip, scrape the "caviar"—the sticky, fragrant seeds—out of the bean into a clean, odorless glass jar. Chop the beans coarsely, and add them to the jar as well. Pour the vodka over the beans, cover tightly, and write the date on the jar. Shake the jar, then wrap it in brown paper (or tuck into a brown paper bag), and store in a cool, dark place.

Shake the jar daily for a week, checking that the tiny seeds remain submerged in the alcohol before you wrap the jar and put it back on the shelf. After the first week, continue to shake the jar a couple of times a week for the remainder of the steeping process. After 8 weeks, your vanilla extract is ready for use.

The beans can remain in the extract for up to about 5 months without deterioration. However, eventually the solids will need to be filtered out via a small sieve, or else they will begin to dissolve.

HOW TO STORE IT Wrapped in brown paper, this extract will keep indefinitely in your pantry.

worcestershire sauce

Makes about 1 1/2 cups

TIME COMMITMENT
about 2 weeks

Tangy, vinegary, and slightly hot and sweet: whether it's used for Bloody Marys or on a steak, this classic sauce cannot be replaced. And it's so easy to make your own. Bottled and wrapped in brown paper, it's a manly, old-school kitchen and bar staple that's giftable and will last for months. Cook's note: tamarind paste can be purchased at Latin American and Asian markets; find fish sauce at Asian markets.

1/2 cup tamarind paste

3 shallots, thinly sliced

1 thin slice fresh ginger

3 cloves

1/2 teaspoon kosher salt

1/4 teaspoon ground nutmeg

3 whole jalapeño chiles, thinly sliced

2 tablespoons plus 2 teaspoons fish sauce

1 tablespoon blackstrap molasses

1/4 cup white distilled vinegar

2 tablespoons corn syrup

1 clove garlic, smashed

1/4 teaspoon black pepper

1 tablespoon dark brown sugar

INSTRUCTIONS Put the tamarind in a medium bowl, add 2/3 cup of warm water, and let sit for 10 minutes. Using your bare hands, squish the paste and water together into a liquid slurry. Remove and discard all seeds and pods.

In a large, clean, odorless jar with a tight lid, combine the tamarind slurry with all the remaining ingredients, plus 1/4 cup of water, and stir or shake to blend. Wrap the jar in brown paper or enclose in a brown paper bag and store in a cool, dark place for 2 weeks to allow the flavors to develop. Shake the contents of the jar every few days.

After 2 weeks, strain the contents of the jar through a fine-mesh sieve set over a bowl, pressing hard on the solids to harvest as much liquid as you can. Discard the solids. Using a funnel, pour the Worcestershire sauce into a pour-top or shaker-top bottle. Label and date the jar. Note that the liquid will settle and become more cloudy on the bottom; this is just the natural characteristic of the brew.

HOW TO STORE IT The sauce will keep for 1 year covered in brown paper in a cool, dark spot in your pantry.

vinegar

Vinegar can be a bit of a culinary singing frog, I've found. I've had wine turn sour quickly and perfectly when no one is looking, but when I've actually tried to coax the right bacteria into action to make pure vinegar, progress has been slow or nil. If you have a friend who already makes vinegar and who can spare a hunk of their "mother"—the large, spongy spore that turns all things alcoholic (red wine, white wine, cider) into vinegar—then stop reading and just do what they tell you to do. If you're truly starting from scratch, however, you need to procure our bacterial friend *Mycoderma aceti* to catalyze the wine. (As a bonus, you will grow your own mother to create more vinegar later.) Find *M. aceti* at your local beer brewing supply shop or online—for example, at Beer-Winemaking.com. (In this recipe, I've adapted Northampton Beer & Winemaking's instructions.) Cook's notes: I've had vinegar happen in as little as five weeks, but three months is not an unusual conversion time. Also, you can use any kind of wine here, but keep in mind that the finished result will still have some of the flavor characteristics of the wine you started with. Don't be put off by homemade vinegar's funky aromas. Because it is unpasteurized, it is a living pantry organism, and its flavor and smell will continue to change as it ages.

12 ounces liquid vinegar starter (*Mycoderma aceti*)
2 cups white or red wine
1 cup water

INSTRUCTIONS Combine all the ingredients in a large earthen crock, a glass jar with a wide top, or a food-grade plastic bucket. Loosely cover the top of the vessel with a thin kitchen towel and tie the towel around the top to secure it. The idea here is to allow airflow in, but keep insects and debris out.

Store the vessel in a warm, dark place and let it sit, undisturbed, for 1 to 3 months. The liquid will grow more cloudy, a sheen will gather at the top, and eventually, a "mother"—a spongy, mushroomlike object—will form on the surface. Strain the vinegar, reserving the mother. Bottle it, date it, and it's ready to use. Additionally, the mother can be used instead of liquid starter to grow additional batches of vinegar (using the same recipe as above). Simply add wine to water in a ratio of 2:1 and begin the process again.

HOW TO STORE IT The vinegar will last in a cool, dark place almost indefinitely. Note that your mother must be "fed" constantly to keep it alive.

PLUS: infused vinegar

Makes about 1 cup

A vinegar infusion is just a gussied-up way of saying flavored vinegar, and it's a great ready-made flavoring condiment for salads, marinades, or anywhere you'd reach for salad dressing. Wild or mild, the flavor possibilities are endless.

INSTRUCTIONS In a clean, odorless container with a tight lid, pour 1 cup of mild white wine, red wine, or apple cider vinegar (either homemade or store-bought) over 1 1/2 cups of packed, lightly crushed fresh herbs, such as cilantro, shiso leaf (found in Japanese markets), basil, or mint. Cap tightly, label and date the jar, and store in a cool, dark place. Swirl the contents of the jar every other day or so for 2 weeks.

After 2 weeks, filter the vinegar through a fine-mesh sieve set over a bowl, pressing on the solids to harvest as much of the vinegar as possible. If your plan is to gift the vinegar, pour it into an insanely attractive bottle and garnish with a couple of sprigs of fresh herbs, either inside or outside the bottle. If you're keeping it for your own use, a pourable bottle or one with a shaker top is a great idea. Stored in a cool, dark place, your vinegar will keep shelf-stable for a year.

Other infusions I have enjoyed include: the zest of 4 large oranges; 5 jalapeño chiles sliced lengthwise, plus 1/2 teaspoon of liquid smoke; and 1 cup chopped sweet apple, the white of a green onion, 2 star anise, and a slice of fresh ginger. Note that you can use vinegars with a strong flavor, such as balsamic and some bold red wine vinegars, but that these strong flavors will remain in the finished infusion.

basic barbecue sauce

Makes about 2 cups

TIME COMMITMENT
about 15 minutes

Some cuisines just inspire fanaticism, and many pray at the Church of Meat and Fire with a religious devotion that I cannot even begin to touch. For you, my pious carnivores, heaps of books and blogs and entire television networks exist to discuss and analyze the dozens of global barbecue styles and sauces—you likely have already found them. For the rest of us who just crave a great plate of ribs and chicken every so often, this is the kind of sweet and tangy red sauce that my mom used to buy in a bottle to douse on chicken wings under the broiler, and it makes me salivate to this day.

2 tablespoons neutral vegetable oil

1 cup minced yellow onion

2 teaspoons kosher salt

2 cloves garlic, minced

1 (6-ounce) can tomato paste

3 tablespoons Worcestershire sauce, either homemade (page 31) or store-bought

5 teaspoons prepared yellow mustard

2 tablespoons blackstrap molasses

1/4 cup plus 1 tablespoon white distilled vinegar

3 tablespoons light brown sugar

1 teaspoon soy sauce

1 teaspoon adobo sauce, either homemade (page 93) or canned

Pinch of black pepper

INSTRUCTIONS In a medium saucepan over medium heat, heat the oil until shimmering. Add the onion and the salt, stir to coat the onion in the oil, and cook until it softens, about 2 minutes. Add the garlic and sauté for another 3 minutes, until fragrant. Stir in the tomato paste and cook for 2 to 3 minutes, until it caramelizes slightly.

Take the pan off the heat and stir in the Worcestershire sauce, mustard, molasses, vinegar, sugar, soy sauce, adobo sauce, and pepper. Transfer the barbecue sauce to a glass jar with a tight-fitting lid.

HOW TO STORE IT Kept refrigerated, it will last for at least 4 months.

smoke and chocolate spice rub

Makes about 3/4 cup

TIME COMMITMENT
about 15 minutes

Looking for something interesting to do with meat? Try this rub on for size. The flavors come together into sort of a dry *mole*. This is masterful on seared tri-tip and pork chops, but it also works well on grilled chicken leg quarters. If you're not a big fan of spicy eats, cut the amount of adobo sauce in half and replace it with an equal amount of orange juice. If your plan is to gift this paste for later use (or just to use it later yourself), omit the garlic and stir it in when you're ready to eat. The other components of the rub can be combined ahead of time, and will last about two weeks.

3 tablespoons unsweetened cocoa powder

2 tablespoons adobo sauce, either homemade (page 93) or canned

1/2 teaspoon ground cinnamon

4 tablespoons freshly squeezed orange juice (from 1 orange)

1 teaspoon orange zest

2 teaspoons salt

3 cloves garlic, minced

INSTRUCTIONS Stir all the ingredients together in a bowl. To use, rub onto 2 pounds of meat. Allow the meat to marinate in the rub, uncovered in the refrigerator, for 30 minutes or more. Grill, pan-sear, roast, or broil the meat as you like.

HOW TO STORE IT To store, spoon the rub into a jar and seal tightly. The rub will keep in the refrigerator for up to 3 days (or 2 weeks if you omit the garlic until you're ready to use the rub).

curry powder

That crazy spice blend you buy in a jar makes for a fast dinner; make it yourself, and it also makes a great quickie gift. I know cookbooks always tell you to use fresh spices for everything, but when it comes to curry powder, this really is An Important Thing. It's also helpful if all of your spices are about the same age and strength for a well-balanced blend. If you have a dedicated coffee mill for grinding fresh spices, this is the time to bust it out—grind as many of the spices as you can fresh (though the onion powder and the garlic powder will need to come ready-made from a big ol' grocery store).

2 tablespoons ground turmeric

5 teaspoons ground cumin

2 teaspoons ground black pepper

1/2 teaspoon ground coriander

1/4 teaspoon ground nutmeg

1/4 teaspoon powdered mustard

1/4 teaspoon ground fennel seeds

1/2 teaspoon kosher salt

1 1/2 teaspoons ground cinnamon

1/4 teaspoon ground cardamom

Pinch of ground cloves

1 teaspoon garlic powder

2 1/2 teaspoons onion powder

1/4 teaspoon cayenne pepper

INSTRUCTIONS Combine all the ingredients in a bowl and mix together with a fork. Using a funnel, pour the mixture into a small glass jar with a tight-fitting lid. Label and date the jar.

HOW TO STORE IT The curry will keep on the shelf for up to 9 months.

PLUS: chicken curry

Serves 3 to 4

What does one do with curry powder? A whisper of it in baked goods, over popcorn, or on eggs is sublime, but for a taste of the classics, try this!

3 tablespoons butter

1 tablespoon neutral vegetable oil

1 yellow onion, chopped

2 teaspoons chopped fresh ginger

2 cloves garlic, minced

3 tablespoons curry powder, homemade (opposite page) or store-bought

1 pound boneless chicken, chopped into bite-size pieces

2 cups chopped fresh or canned tomatoes (page 27), chicken stock, water, or coconut milk (page 120)

1 cup fresh or thawed frozen peas

4 cups cooked rice

INSTRUCTIONS In a deep sauté pan or Dutch oven, heat the butter and oil over medium heat. Add the onion and sauté until soft, about 3 minutes. Add the ginger and garlic and cook, stirring constantly, 3 minutes more. Add the curry powder and allow the spices to toast for 1 minute. Add the chicken and the tomatoes and stir well to combine, scraping up all of the browned bits from the bottom of the pan.

Cover, reduce the heat to medium-low, and allow to gently simmer for 15 minutes. Stir in the peas, cover again, and allow to simmer for 5 minutes more. Serve immediately over rice.

miso

Makes 5 pints

TIME COMMITMENT
about 6 weeks

I used to live in Japan, and I never say no to raw fish or fresh shiso leaves. I've always loved how making Japanese food feels really complicated, but it ain't. File "making miso" under that category. Mush together regular ol' soy beans, sea salt, water, and one special ingredient, Koji rice (rice that has been inoculated with the appropriate fermenting bacteria), set it to rest for about 6 weeks, and voila! A dreamy, salty basis for soups, spreads, fish rubs, and pickles (page 45). Note that this recipe makes a light miso, also called mellow miso or yellow miso, and that it yields plenty to share. This has the shortest sitting time of all the misos and is one of the most forgiving (and quickly rewarding) styles. And if you decide to take this one step further and innoculate your own Koji rice, you are much, much cooler than I. If you can't find Koji at your local health food store, you can order it online (I buy mine from GEMCultures.com). Cook's note: You can use any kind of unpasteurized miso to help jump-start your fermentation, either store-bought or from your own previous batch of miso. This is optional, but it will help accelerate the process. For more awesome hardcore miso info, pick up *The Miso Book: The Art of Cooking with Miso* by John Belleme.

1 1/4 pounds dried soybeans (about 3 1/4 cups)

1 1/4 cups sea salt

2 pounds Koji rice (about 5 1/4 cups)

1/4 cup unpasteurized miso (optional)

5 to 6 cups water

INSTRUCTIONS Soak the soybeans in 8 cups of water for at least 12 hours but not more than 24. Drain and rinse the beans thoroughly.

In a large covered stock pot or Dutch oven, cover the beans with water by 2 inches. Cover, bring to a boil, and then reduce the heat to a simmer for about 3 1/2 hours, stirring from time to time, until the beans are soft and tender to the bite. Err on the side of overcooked rather than under.

Drain and rinse the beans. Mash them with a potato masher or ricer.

Transfer the bean puree to a very large bowl or mixing vessel, and mix in 1 cup of the salt and the Koji rice, stirring well with a heavy wooden spoon to combine thoroughly.

Dissolve the unpasteurized miso, if using, into 1 cup of water, and stir well to help the miso dissolve. Pour over the soy bean mixture and mix in thoroughly. Add 3 more cups of water (or 4 cups if you've not used the miso slurry) and mix in well. Take a handful of the miso paste and squeeze it in your fist. It should be wet enough to squeeze through your fingers. If not, add the final cup of water and evenly combine.

You will need a clean, large ceramic, glass, or food-grade plastic vessel in which to ferment the miso, and a free-fitting lid large enough to sit on top of the miso and press down on it while its volume shrinks. Evenly sprinkle 2 tablespoons of the salt over the bottom of the container and pour in a quarter of the miso, packing it down firmly with your clean hand or the back of a spoon. Gently but firmly, twist, shake, bang, or tap the container to release any air bubbles. Continue to add the miso in small batches and continue to pack it as tightly as possible.

Once all the miso is packed and the air bubbles have been removed, sprinkle the final 2 tablespoons of salt evenly over the top. Lay plastic wrap on top of the miso to the edges, and then place the lid directly on top of the miso, not on top of the container itself. Add a weight, such as a pint jar filled with water or a 28-ounce can, on top of the miso. Cover the whole kit and kaboodle with a clean dish towel and tie it with string to keep it secure—just enough to keep out dust and insects.

Mark the container with today's date and the dates for 2 weeks, 4 weeks, and 6 weeks out. Go put these dates on your calendar so that you remember to check on your miso. Go ahead. I'll wait. Let the miso sit in a warm, but not hot, place to ferment.

After 2 weeks, check on your miso. Send a spoon deep below the top salted surface of the miso and taste. The aroma should be kind of sweet and fermented and somewhat alcoholic, pleasant and unpleasant at the same time. Unless the weather has been very warm, it likely won't be ready for another month. But if you'd like a stronger flavor, let it sit for 8 weeks, testing deep below the surface weekly until the flavor suits you.

Once the miso is to your liking, scrape off the top $1/2$ to $3/4$ inch of the miso and discard. Stir the remaining miso well; it will be salty and its aroma should be pleasant. Your miso is ready to eat, and it should look quite "inaka style"—country style and sort of chunky. If you prefer a completely smooth paste, puree it in the food processor in batches for 3 minutes.

Pack the finished miso into pint jars with an inch or more of space on top (the miso will expand), labeling and dating them.

HOW TO STORE IT Kept refrigerated, the miso will be fresh, but ever-changing, for 9 months. Note that miso is a fermented food, so it should not be canned.

4 pickle it

Sweet pickles, sour pickles, fermented pickles, vinegar pickles, salt pickles . . . baby, I ♥ pickles. A true sucker for anything that makes me pucker, I have never met a pickled vegetable I didn't like. I say, if you have pickles, you always have something to eat.

While many people associate pickling with summer produce, I've tried to focus on some of the least-loved players in the pickle pyramid, homing in on winter's bounty and those produce-aisle beauties with a long and hearty growing season. I've also tried to provide a wide swath of flavors, from sweet to tangy to salty.

In short, I am on a serious quest to bring back the relish tray. And why not? A little chopping, a few days' wait, and you have an aesthetically pleasing, colorful condiment that goes with almost everything, from the usuals—like sandwiches, salads, and roast meats—to some surprises, like tacos, pizza, and omelets.

Now, say this ten times fast: preserve your palate and your pantry with the pleasing pucker of pickles.

sweet pepper and corn relish

Makes about 6 cups
(3 pints)

TIME COMMITMENT
about 1 day

I drink the brine on this one. I kid you not. This is a super old-fashioned pickle so self-consciously retro that it's modern again—ready for its place on your Aunt Bitty's relish tray alongside the three-bean salad and the pickled beets. Just FYI, I actually prefer frozen corn to fresh here because—well, forgive my shallowness, but frozen corn is just prettier than anything I've ever been able to cut off the cob, and the strong flavors in this mix don't merit the extra effort. (Oh, and thanks to my intern, Sam, who showed me how awesome this is baked with salami on a pizza.) Note that it's natural for the brine to get cloudy as the corn releases its starch.

1 tablespoon vegetable oil

3 3/4 cups diced red bell pepper (3 or 4 peppers)

1 tablespoon kosher salt

4 cups fresh or thawed frozen corn kernels

1 3/4 cups diced red onion (1 very large onion)

1 1/2 cups apple cider vinegar

1 1/2 cups sugar

1/2 teaspoon ground turmeric

INSTRUCTIONS Heat the oil in a large skillet over medium-high heat. Add the peppers and salt and sauté for approximately 12 minutes, stirring often, until the peppers soften and begin to caramelize. Add the corn, stirring to combine, and cook the vegetables for 3 to 4 minutes longer, until the corn is hot. Turn off the heat and add the onion to the pan; stir well.

In a small saucepan over medium heat, combine the vinegar, sugar, and turmeric and stir just until the sugar dissolves, about 2 minutes.

Pack the vegetables tightly into 3 clean pint jars, and pour the warm brine over the vegetables to cover completely, discarding any unused brine. To can the relish for longer storage, process the jars according to the instructions on page 28. Otherwise, cover tightly, and let the relish sit at room temperature for 1 day before moving it to the refrigerator.

HOW TO STORE IT Refrigerated, this will keep for up to 6 months. Canned, it will keep for up to 1 year.

ploughman's pickle

Makes about 8 cups

TIME COMMITMENT
about 3 hours

And what, you're asking, is ploughman's pickle? Well, it's a killer British condiment traditionally part of a ploughman's lunch—the quintessential pub grub: bread, cheese, meat, pickled onions, and this awesome, tangy, sweet condiment (it often travels under the brand name Branston Pickle). Tuck it into a Cheddar cheese sandwich. Thank me later. Most of the time you spend making this will be you getting supercozy and comfortable with your knife and cutting board. A fine, fine chop—not quite a mince, but not a thoughtless cubing, either—is really the only way to get the texture just right. Also, don't let the tamarind paste put you off. It's a frequent staple found in almost any Indian, Vietnamese, Thai, or Latin American grocery.

1/2 cup tamarind paste

3 1/2 cups apple cider vinegar

2 cups sugar

16 dates, finely chopped (about 2 cups)

1 large sweet apple, peeled, cored, and chopped (about 1 1/2 cups)

1 tablespoon kosher salt

4 cloves garlic, minced

1 1/2 cups finely diced carrot

1 cup finely diced cauliflower, mostly stems

1 cup finely diced zucchini

1 cup finely diced red onion

INSTRUCTIONS Whew! That was a lot of chopping. Now, let's make the brine.

Put the tamarind in a medium bowl, add 1 cup warm water, and let sit for 10 minutes. Using your bare hands, squish the paste and water together into a liquid slurry. Remove and discard all seeds and pods.

In a large, covered saucepan or Dutch oven, combine the tamarind slurry, vinegar, sugar, dates, apple, salt, and garlic. Bring to a boil over high heat, then reduce the heat and simmer, uncovered, for 30 minutes, mashing the fruit with a wooden spoon or potato masher as it softens. Once the volume of the liquid has reduced by about half and the mixture has become thick and syrupy, turn off the heat. Add the carrot, cauliflower, zucchini, and onion and stir to coat completely. Allow the vegetables to rest in the pot, covered, for 1 hour.

HOW TO STORE IT Pack the pickle into clean glass jars and refrigerate for up to 3 months. Or pack it into sterile canning jars and process for 15 minutes (review the instructions on page 28). This will keep for up to 1 year on the shelf.

miso pickles

Makes 2 cups

TIME COMMITMENT
about 5 days

The salt and living enzymes of miso slowly work magic on the daikon to craft a pickle that's supercrunchy and pleasantly full-flavored, with a different texture than vinegar pickles. Oh, and don't let the use of mirin throw you. It's just a sweet Japanese cooking wine available at many Asian markets. You can easily substitute carrots, turnips, or other radishes or firm root vegetables for the daikon, but I don't recommend this pickling theater for more watery vegetables like cucumbers. Note also that this is a fermented pickle and therefore it should not be canned.

2 tablespoons mirin

1 clove garlic, minced

1/2 cup miso (either homemade, from page 38, or store-bought)

1/2 pound daikon, peeled and sliced into 1/4-inch half-moons (about 2 cups)

INSTRUCTIONS In a medium mixing bowl, stir the mirin and garlic into the miso to combine. Add the daikon to the bowl and, using a rubber spatula, fold it into the miso mixture, taking care to coat each piece of daikon completely. Note that the pickle may seem pasty and dry, depending on your miso. Fear not; it will release liquid as it cures.

Transfer the pickle to a clean wide-mouthed pint jar with a well-fitting lid, using your hands to help press the pickle into the jar. Label and date the jar, and allow it to sit at room temperature for 24 hours, then move it to the refrigerator for 4 days. Your pickle will now be ready to eat. Some people prefer to rinse off the clinging miso brine before eating, whereas I like its sharp saltiness all around. Be sure to try it both ways.

HOW TO STORE IT Kept refrigerated, this pickle will last (and, in fact, get better) for up to 3 months.

pickled grapes

Makes about 2 cups

TIME COMMITMENT
3 to 7 days

Look out, cocktail onion! These tangy, sweet roundies are a fine cocktail garnish: string three together on a toothpick and you have instant fancy-schmancy. They're also delicious served as a relish alongside roast chicken. If you're going to gift these, do so when they're freshly packed. They will remain delicious over time, but the color will suffer.

1 clove garlic, peeled and smashed

3 cloves

1 (2-inch) piece green onion (from the white part)

1 (2-inch) cinnamon stick

1 (1/4-inch) slice fresh ginger

2 cups seedless grapes, stemmed and washed

2 tablespoons sugar

1 teaspoon kosher salt

1/3 cup plus 2 tablespoons white distilled vinegar, plus more as needed

1/3 cup plus 1 tablespoon water, plus more as needed

INSTRUCTIONS Drop the garlic, cloves, green onion, cinnamon, and ginger into the bottom of a clean pint jar with a tight-fitting lid. Add the grapes to the jar, packing them tightly without crushing. (Shaking the jar from time to time will assist with this process.)

Sprinkle on the sugar and salt, and pour in the vinegar (if it doesn't fill the jar halfway, feel free to add a little more). Next, pour in the water (topping off if necessary to completely cover the fruit). Secure the lid tightly and shake the jar gently to dissolve the salt and sugar.

Let sit out on the countertop for 3 days or inside the refrigerator for 1 week, shaking the jar gently daily to distribute the flavors.

HOW TO STORE IT Refrigerated, these will keep for up to 1 year.

5 bake it

How many packages of prefab bread products would you guesstimate that you've purchased in your lifetime? Got it? Okay, now double it. Yeah, that's probably about right. Though a handful of us yeast geeks might take a Saturday afternoon to lovingly craft a loaf or two of the crustiest bread that our cool home ovens will allow, few of us think about practical baking in the long term: stocking the freezer with the morning carbs (bagels or English muffins) to sustain us Monday through Friday, or putting forth the effort to whip up the buns for summer barbecues, or making our own pizza dough and having it at the ready in the freezer.

A bag of flour and a handful of your effort are the bulk of what's needed to add your stamp to some of the best and most versatile kitchen baked goods at a fraction of the cost of the store-bought stuff. No twist-tie required: the recipes that follow are all you "knead" to strut your yeasty stuff.

bagels

Makes 12 bagels

TIME COMMITMENT
less than 3 hours

Chewy, dense, and round (duh!), these are not mammoth bagels-on-steroids, but they are flavor giants to be reckoned with. The best thing about making your own? Poppy seeds and salt on both sides! (But, of course, you can stud them with whatever you desire.) • Bagels must be boiled, and you simply can't skip that step. And don't hate me for making you hunt down malt powder; find it at beer brewing stores, health food stores, or online (for example, at Amazon.com or KingArthurFlour.com). In a total pinch, you can substitute brown sugar, but it's just not the same.

5 cups (1 pound, 11 ounces) all-purpose flour, plus more as needed

1 tablespoon kosher salt

1 packet (2 1/2 teaspoons) active dry yeast

1 tablespoon nondiastatic malt powder

1 3/4 cups water

BOILING BATH

9 cups water

2 tablespoons nondiastatic malt powder

1 teaspoon baking soda

1 egg white

Flaky finishing salt, poppy seeds, or sesame seeds

INSTRUCTIONS In a food processor or stand mixer fitted with the dough blade, combine the flour, salt, yeast, and malt powder. With the machine running, slowly stream in the 1 3/4 cups of water. The dough will come together in a solid mass. Allow the machine to knead the dough for 2 to 4 minutes, until a stiff and cohesive dough forms.

Transfer the dough to a countertop lightly dusted with flour and continue to knead, pushing the ball in from the sides and then over the top from the bottom. Add more flour as needed, a tablespoon at a time, if the dough is wet and sticky. After 5 to 8 minutes of kneading, the cracks in the dough should smooth out and it should become as pliant as an earlobe.

Place the dough in a lightly oiled bowl and cover the bowl with a clean, damp kitchen towel. Heat a cup of water in the microwave for 1 minute and remove. Place the covered dough bowl in the warm, moist microwave and let sit for 1 hour. (Or let the dough rise in another warm, moist place.)

About 15 minutes before the hour is up, make the boiling bath. Combine the water, malt powder, and baking soda in a wide, heavy Dutch oven or stockpot. Cover the pot and bring to a vigorous boil over high heat.

Preheat the oven to 425°F and line 2 large baking sheets with parchment paper.

Lightly flour the countertop again and put the dough on it. Roll the dough into a ball with your hands. Stick

// CONTINUED

your finger directly into the center to make a small hole. Use your fingers to widen the hole and work the dough, hand over hand as if you're pulling on a rope, into a large O-shape about 2 inches thick. Look! A giant bagel!

Cut the rope in half, then cut each half in half again; you will have 4 equal parts. Cut each piece into thirds, resulting in 12 dough pieces total.

Work with one dough ball at a time, leaving the others covered with the damp towel. Roll the dough ball into a sphere, flatten it slightly, and then stick your finger through the center. Widen the hole with your fingers until the bagel reaches about 4 inches across (it will puff up a bit more after being boiled). Try to ensure that the dough has the same thickness all the way around the hole; this allows for even cooking. Put the shaped bagel on one of the prepared baking sheets and shape 5 more, for a total of 6. (Leave the remaining dough pieces under the towel.)

Once your boiling bath is boiling rapidly, have two utensils, such as a slotted spoon and a wooden spoon, at the ready to help get your bagels into and out of the bath quickly. Place 3 bagels into the bath and boil for 1 minute. Use your utensils to turn them over, and boil for 1 minute more. Remove the bagels one at a time, holding them over

the bath to drain them well, and transfer them back to the baking sheet. Repeat with the other 3 bagels.

Beat the egg white with 1 teaspoon of water and brush each boiled bagel with the egg white mixture, and then top with as little or as much as you like of the salt and seeds. If you desire, flip the bagels over, brush with more egg mixture, and add more toppings.

Move the sheet of bagels into the oven and bake for 12 minutes. Take the bagels from the oven, flip them over, and then bake for 6 minutes more, until they are lightly browned and shiny all over. Transfer them to a rack and allow them to cool completely, at least 30 minutes.

While the first batch of 6 bagels is in the oven, shape, boil, and salt/seed the remaining 6 bagels, using the other prepared baking sheet.

The bagels' full texture does not develop until they have fully cooled. These are best if eaten the same day, but they are still delicious split and toasted the next day.

HOW TO STORE IT Put the bagels in a zip-top bag, force out as much air as you can, seal, and freeze for up to 6 months. Thaw at room temperature for about 4 hours before slicing and toasting.

english muffins

Makes 12 muffins

TIME COMMITMENT
about 2 hours

Next time you come over for brunch, I'll make eggs, squeeze some juice, thaw out some homemade bacon, and, uh-huh, that's right: I'll make English muffins. And when I come to your house, you can, too. These are dense, chewy canvases ready to accept your butter, jam, hollandaise, and so on. Their flavor is top-notch, and they freeze like a dream.

1 packet (2 1/2 teaspoons) active dry yeast

3 1/2 cups (1 pound, 4 ounces) bread flour, plus more as needed

1 tablespoon sugar

1 teaspoon kosher salt

1 teaspoon white distilled vinegar

3/4 cup milk

1 tablespoon butter, softened

3/4 cup water

INSTRUCTIONS In a food processor fitted with the dough blade, pulse together the yeast, flour, sugar, and salt. In a cup or small bowl, mix together the vinegar and milk. With the machine running, slowly pour in the milk mixture, and drop in the butter. Pour the water through the tube slowly as the dough forms. Allow the machine to knead the dough for 5 to 8 minutes, until the dough pulls cleanly away from the sides of the work bowl. If the dough is too sticky, add more flour, 1 tablespoon at a time. Transfer the dough to a lightly floured countertop, roll it into a ball, and put it in a large, lightly oiled bowl. Cover the bowl with a clean, damp kitchen towel. Warm one cup of water in the microwave for 1 minute, then remove. Place the covered dough bowl in the warm, moist microwave and let sit for 1 hour. (Or let the dough rise in another warm, moist place.)

Lightly flour your work surface again and put the dough on it. Roll the dough into a ball with your hands. Stick your finger directly into the center to make a small hole. Use your fingers to widen the hole and work the dough, hand over hand as if you're pulling on a rope, into a large O-shape about 2 inches thick. Cut the circle and shape it into a rope about 36 inches long. Cut the rope in half, then cut each half in half again; you will have 4 equal parts. Cut each piece into thirds, resulting in 12 dough pieces total. Roll each piece of dough into a ball and cover with a damp towel.

Heat a griddle or a heavy skillet over medium to medium-low heat. Once it's hot, lightly oil the pan. Pick up a ball of dough and slap it between your hands to form a patty 1/2 to 3/4 inch thick, place on the griddle, and cook for 3 minutes per side, until the muffin puffs and turns brown (not black!). Add as many muffins to your pan as you can without crowding—about 3 for a standard skillet, or up to 8 at a time on a griddle. Remove the muffin from the griddle and transfer to a plate or cooling rack. Let the muffins rest for at least 15 minutes; this is critical for achieving the proper texture. For the ultimate "nook and cranny" experience, don't slice the muffin open. Instead, perforate the perimeter of the muffin with the tines of a fork and split it by hand.

HOW TO STORE IT These are best if eaten fresh, but they are also delicious split and toasted the next day. Beyond that, put in a zip-top bag, force out as much air as you can, seal, and freeze: they will remain cryogenically delicious for up to 1 year.

hamburger buns and hot dog buns

Makes 12 buns

TIME COMMITMENT
about 2 hours

If you're going to go to all the trouble of making your own 'gers and dogs, and you're striving to be teacher's pet by rustling up your own ketchup, mustard, and mayo, doesn't that DIY BBQ deserve this final capstone in the food geek pyramid? These soft, white, tiny loaves are the perfect vessels to receive your best grilled meats, lobster salads, or cold-cut extravaganzas: in short, they're ready for any sort of oddly shaped sandwich situation.

5 cups (1 pound, 11 ounces) all-purpose flour, plus more for dusting

2 packets (5 teaspoons) active dry yeast

2 tablespoons sugar

1 tablespoon kosher salt

2 tablespoons butter, softened

1 cup milk, plus more for brushing

1 cup water

INSTRUCTIONS In a food processor fitted with the plastic dough blade, pulse together the flour, yeast, sugar, and salt until combined. Add the butter and process until it's thoroughly incorporated. With the machine running, stream in the milk and the water. Once the dough forms into a ball, turn it onto a lightly floured countertop and knead for about 1 minute, just until it comes together and the outside is no longer sticky. Transfer the dough to a lightly oiled large bowl and cover the bowl with a damp, clean kitchen towel. Heat a cup of water in the microwave for 1 minute and remove. Place the covered dough bowl in the warm, moist microwave and let sit for 1 hour. Lightly oil 2 baking sheets.

Lightly flour your countertop again and put the dough on it. Roll the dough into a ball with your hands. Stick your finger directly into the center to make a small hole. Use your fingers to widen the hole and work the dough, hand over hand as if you're pulling on a rope, into a large O-shape about 2 inches thick. Cut the rope in half, then cut each half in half again; you will have 4 equal parts. Cut each piece into thirds, resulting in 12 dough pieces total.

Keep the dough pieces covered under a moist towel to keep them from drying out while you work. One at a time, roll each piece into a ball. For burger buns, press down on the dough ball to flatten its bottom. For hot dog buns, pinch, stretch, and shape the dough into 7-inch-long rolls. Transfer the buns to the baking sheets as you form them, evenly spacing 6 buns per sheet. Let the dough rest on the baking sheets for 30 minutes.

Preheat the oven to 400°F. Brush the tops of the buns with milk, place both sheets in the oven, and bake for 10 minutes. Rotate each baking sheet 90 degrees and switch racks (so that the topmost baking sheet moves to the bottom rack and vice versa). Bake for 10 minutes more, or until the tops are golden brown (take care not to let the bottoms get too dark). Let cool slightly before serving.

HOW TO STORE IT These are best if eaten the same day, or you can serve them toasted for up to 2 days after baking. Or wrap tightly in plastic wrap, place in a zip-top bag, force out as much air as you can, and seal: these can be frozen for up to 6 months.

pizza dough

Let's be honest. Unless you're fortunate enough to have a snazzy oven that can crank to nearly 1,000 degrees, the pizza you make at home will not replicate the pies from your favorite *pizzaiolo*. That said, you can certainly roll out something that's still entirely worth the effort. The trick is to let the dough sit overnight, which vastly improves the texture and chew.

1 packet (2$1/2$ teaspoons) active dry yeast

3$1/4$ cups (1 pound, 2 ounces) all-purpose flour, plus more for dusting

1 tablespoon plus 2 teaspoons kosher salt

1 tablespoon dried rosemary

1 tablespoon olive oil

1$1/2$ cups water

INSTRUCTIONS In a food processor fitted with the dough blade (or a stand mixer fitted with the dough hook), whirl together the yeast, flour, salt, and rosemary. With the motor running (at medium speed for a stand mixer), drizzle in the oil, then the water, until a dough forms. Keep the machine running for 2 to 3 minutes to knead the dough—it will slap around the sides of the bowl, so hang onto your machine and enjoy the ride. The dough will be warm when you take it from the machine.

To make the dough by hand, mix together the dry ingredients in a large bowl. Mix in the oil and water, starting with a spoon and then using your hands. Turn the dough out onto a floured work surface and knead for about 10 minutes, until the dough is slightly shiny, and smooth and firm like an earlobe.

Lightly oil a large bowl. Roll the dough into a ball, place it in the bowl, and turn it once to coat with the oil. Cover the bowl with a damp, clean kitchen towel (don't allow the towel to touch the dough). Heat a cup of water in the microwave for 1 minute and remove. Place the covered dough bowl in the warm, moist microwave and let sit for at least 8 and up to 24 hours. (Or let the dough rise in another warm, moist place.)

When the dough has risen, pull it away from the sides of the bowl and transfer it to a floured work surface, rolling it into a ball. Cut the dough into 4 equal pieces. Roll each piece into a ball, and use or store.

HOW TO STORE IT The dough can be refrigerated for up to 1 week or frozen, wrapped twice in plastic wrap and stored in an airtight container, for up to 6 months. Thaw in the refrigerator for 24 hours before using.

PLUS: pizza

Makes four 8-inch pizzas

Don't be trepidatious about toppings. Ditch the sauce and cheese in favor of ricotta and olives, corn relish and salami, pesto and vegetables—or fruit slices and sugar.

Pizza Dough (opposite page)
Olive oil, for brushing
3/4 cup marinara sauce
6 ounces mozzarella cheese, shredded or cut into strips
Finishing salt

INSTRUCTIONS Position an oven rack in the center of the oven and preheat to 500°F. Lightly oil 2 rimmed baking sheets.

Work with 1 ball of dough at a time, keeping the others covered with a damp kitchen towel. Dust a work surface with flour and, using a rolling pin (or a wine bottle), roll out a ball of dough to a 9-inch round. Gently transfer the dough round to one side of one of the baking sheets and crimp the edges with your fingers, lightly twisting as you go, to make an 8-inch pizza with crust. Roll out the remaining 3 balls of dough and move them to the baking sheets as well, so that you end up with 2 rounds per sheet.

Brush each pizza with olive oil. Spoon on 3 tablespoons of sauce, smoothing it evenly to the crust's edge. Sprinkle on 1/4 of the cheese and finishing salt to taste.

Bake 1 sheet of pizzas at a time for 9 minutes. Rotate the sheet and bake for about 9 minutes more, until the crust is golden brown and very dark brown in spots. Bake the second tray of pizzas in the same way. Serve immediately.

cakes in a jar

If you can boil canning jars and use them for drinking lemonade, why not use them as a vessel for the cutest single-serving cake/pudding thing ever? Simply screw on the lid and you have a portable picnic food at the ready. Hurray! I devised this concoction in summer; hence the summer fruit. But I encourage you to use 2 1/2 cups total of whatever fruit is in right now. This is also a good use for less-than-perfect fruit.

1 1/2 cups pitted cherries

1 cup sliced strawberries

1/2 cup all-purpose flour

1/2 cup sugar

1/2 teaspoon salt

4 tablespoons butter

3/4 cup heavy whipping cream

INSTRUCTIONS Preheat the oven to 350°F.

In a small bowl, combine the cherries and strawberries and divide the fruit evenly among 4 half-pint canning jars. In another bowl, whisk together the flour, sugar, and salt and divide the mixture among the jars (1/4 cup per jar), tapping and shaking well to distribute the dry ingredients around the fruit. Top each jar with 1 tablespoon of butter. Note that the jars will not be filled all the way.

Fill the bottom of an 8-inch square or round baking dish with dried beans in at least a double layer. Nestle each jar flat on its bottom in the pan; the jars should not be touching one another. (The beans will help keep the jars steady while you're moving them in and out of the oven.)

Bake for 1 hour, until the tops are brown and bubbly and the cakes have set. Allow the cakes to cool on a rack for 20 minutes.

Whip the cream in a stand mixer or using a hand mixer until soft peaks form. Dollop whipped cream on each of the cakes and serve. Eat straight out of the jars.

HOW TO STORE IT These can be made ahead; stored (with a proper lid and sans whipped cream) in the refrigerator for up to 1 week; and, need I say, gifted.

6 | stalk it

Corn is a glorious thing. It has a long history as a dietary staple, and it's a shape-shifter in the kitchen, versatile and agile in a wide array of preparations. Lately it has also become a bumpy yellow magnet for food politics, inspiring a double handful of books and movies. Let us take a moment to simply appreciate corn in all of its abundance and importance.

Done appreciating? Good! Now, let's cut to the grind and get eating. Corn dough, aka masa, is the start of many wonderful meals—from tacos to tamales—and once I started grinding my own, I just couldn't stop. I hope you soon share my obsession.

masa

Makes about 2¹/₂ pounds
(enough for about
32 tortillas or about
30 tamales)

TIME COMMITMENT
about 15 hours

Warning: of all the recipes in this book, this one may very well be the most habit-forming, and it will surely make you steer clear of store-bought tortillas and tamales for all but emergencies. While true Latin American masa (the corn dough that is the start to so many staples) is made from hearty field corn and ground by hand in a stone metate, this version, which uses whole dried corn and a food processor, is a knock-out stand-in for the urban apartment kitchen. Masa freezes like a champ; just add a little extra water to your thawed dough before using. I highly suggest using organic whole corn, which, if you can't find it at your local health food store, can be ordered online at TropicalTraditions.com or through Anson Mills. Note that whole-grain corn is not the same thing as popcorn. Also, calcium hydroxide, a toxic chemical that's necessary to remove the indigestible outer hull of the corn, goes by many names, including "pickling lime," "slaked lime," and the trig and friendly "cal." Buy it online if you can't find it in the grocery store, health food store, or Latin American or Asian grocery. Use caution with this stuff, but don't freak out about it; just wash your hands well after handling it. All of it is washed away long before the corn becomes food. Final cook's note: If you can't find whole dried corn, or if working with calcium hydroxide scares the bejeezus out of you, you can start with dried hominy and prepare it the same way without the lime. It's good, but not as good as whole corn.

2 pounds (about 5¹/₂ cups) whole-grain dried corn kernels
1 tablespoon pickling lime (calcium hydroxide)
4 rounded teaspoons kosher salt

INSTRUCTIONS Wash the corn very well in a colander—do not skip this step. Pour the cleaned corn into a very large stockpot and cover with water by at least 4 inches (the corn will expand later). Remove and discard any floating bits of corn, stirring the corn a couple of times and removing any floaters that rise to the top.

Cover the pot and bring to a boil over high heat. Once the water is boiling, carefully sprinkle the pickling lime over the top and stir it in well; the corn will get bright and sunny. Once the lime is evenly distributed, cover the pot and let it boil for 15 minutes.

After 15 minutes, turn off the heat and let the corn sit for 12 hours or overnight, stirring once or twice.

The next morning, the corn will have expanded and the water will have turned cloudy. Pour the corn through a colander, discarding the liquid, and wash the corn vigorously under running water: pick up large handfuls and rub them together hard, as if you were trying to polish rocks. Be sure to clean all the corn very well: this step eliminates the outer husk and the pickling lime. This cleaning should take 10 to 15 minutes.

Now it's time to grind. Scoop 1 1/2 cups of prepared corn into the bowl of a food processor fitted with the steel blade and blend for 30 seconds. With the machine running, drizzle in 2 tablespoons of water and a rounded teaspoon of kosher salt. Stop the machine, scrape down the sides, scoop in 1/2 cup of corn, and drizzle another tablespoon of water around the perimeter of the bowl. Whirl for 30 seconds. This will produce a masa that still has some chunky pieces of corn and whole corn in it. The texture of the masa will be slightly shaggy, but it will pinch together cohesively and be sort of sticky. If you prefer a totally smooth masa, simply grind together 2 cups of corn, 3 tablespoons of water, and 1 rounded teaspoon of salt for 1 minute. Working in batches, process all of the corn in the same manner, moving the corn dough to a large holding bowl covered with a damp kitchen towel as you work. An odd half-cup of corn can simply be added to the last batch.

Gently knead the dough together in the bowl to form a cohesive mass, then split the masa into 2 equal parts and form into balls. Your masa is now ready to be used or stored. Refrigerated, it will keep for up to 3 days.

HOW TO STORE IT Wrapped twice in plastic and then placed in an airtight container, it can be frozen for up to 3 months. To use, simply thaw at room temperature and knead in a couple of tablespoons of water before using, to get it to a pliant and dough-like consistency.

corn tortillas (two ways)

TIME COMMITMENT
less than 1 hour

If you can make pancakes, you can make tortillas. While truly homemade tortillas require using corn you processed yourself (see opposite page), making your own from masa harina, which is dried masa that has been finely ground, is totally cinchy—akin to making pancakes from a mix. The most popular brand of masa harina is Maseca (widely available at Latin American grocery stores), but I encourage you to go with organic corn products such as Bob's Red Mill, or whatever else is available at your local health food store.

corn tortillas from masa harina

Makes 12 tortillas

2 cups masa harina

1 cup water

1/4 cup vegetable oil, plus more for the pan

2 teaspoons kosher salt

INSTRUCTIONS In a mixing bowl, stir together the masa harina, water, oil, and salt until a dough forms. Let the dough rest for 5 minutes.

Measure 2 tablespoons of the dough and roll it into a ball between your wet hands. Follow suit with the remainder of the dough; you will end up with about a dozen small balls. Meanwhile, heat a griddle (preferable), cast-iron pan, or heavy skillet over medium-high heat.

Working with 1 ball at a time, place it between 2 sheets of parchment paper (wax paper will stick) and flatten with a heavy skillet or saucepan: a twisting "steering wheel" motion works better than just pressing straight down.

The dough will flatten into a pancake about 4 1/2 inches in diameter and 1/8 inch thick. Lightly oil the hot pan.

Lift the tortilla in its paper from the work surface and carefully peel back the paper from one side; let the tortilla fall from the other sheet of paper into your hand. (If the delicate tortilla breaks here, don't sweat it; just re-roll and try again.) Lay it in the pan and cook on one side until the top bubbles and spots of brown char appear on the bottom, about 2 minutes. Flip and cook the other side for 2 minutes more. Feel free to cook more than 1 tortilla at a time, but don't crowd the pan. Oil the pan as needed between batches.

HOW TO STORE IT These are best eaten as soon as they're cooked. They will last refrigerated for up to 5 days; before eating, warm either in a lightly oiled frying pan or by wrapping in wet paper towels and zapping for 10 seconds in the microwave. Tortillas can also be frozen for up to 6 months: wrap tightly in plastic wrap and store in an air-tight container or zip-top bag.

corn tortillas from homemade masa

Makes about 32 tortillas

> 2½ pounds homemade masa (page 62)
> Kosher salt (optional)

INSTRUCTIONS If you're beginning with frozen masa, let it thaw either in the fridge for 24 hours or on the countertop for 8 hours. Unwrap it, move it to a bowl, and add water, 1 tablespoon at a time, to make the masa pliant and dough-like again.

Measure 2 tablespoons of the masa and roll it into a ball between your hands. Follow suit with the remainder of the dough; you will end up with about 32 small balls. Meanwhile, heat a griddle (preferably), cast-iron pan, or heavy skillet over medium-high heat.

Working with 1 ball at a time, place it between 2 sheets of parchment paper (wax paper will stick) and flatten with a heavy skillet or saucepan: a twisting "steering wheel" motion works better than just pressing straight down.

The dough will flatten into a pancake about 4½ inches in diameter and ⅛ inch thick. Lightly oil the hot pan.

Lift the tortilla in its paper from the work surface and carefully peel back the paper from one side; let the tortilla fall from the other sheet of paper into your hand. (If the delicate tortilla breaks here, don't sweat it; just re-roll and try again.) Lay it in the pan and cook on one side until the edges begin to curl up, about 4 minutes. If you like, sprinkle a little more salt on top of the tortilla once it's in the pan. Flip and cook the other side for about 4 minutes more. Feel free to cook more than 1 tortilla at a time, but don't crowd the pan. Oil the pan as needed between batches.

HOW TO STORE IT These are best eaten as soon as they're cooked. They will last refrigerated up to 5 days; before eating, warm either in a lightly oiled frying pan or by wrapping in wet paper towels and zapping for 10 seconds in the microwave. Tortillas can also be frozen for up to 6 months: wrap tightly in plastic wrap and store in an airtight container or zip-top bag.

tortilla chips and tostadas

Makes 60 chips or
10 tostada shells

TIME COMMITMENT
about 45 minutes

Americans fell in love with chips and salsa in the 1990s, and they've never left the table. Make them more comical at your own risk by serving the chips around the brim of a straw hat with a bowl of salsa (like the one in the sidebar) in the middle. If you're making tostadas, top them with your favorite meat, beans, guacamole, cheese, ceviche, and so on. This is a stellar use for stale tortillas. Cook's note: the leftover oil can be cooled, strained, and bottled for later use.

2 cups neutral vegetable oil
10 corn tortillas, homemade (page 64) or store-bought
Kosher salt

INSTRUCTIONS Pour the oil into a heavy 10-inch skillet (the oil should be about 1/2 inch deep). Heat over medium to medium-high heat until the oil shimmers, about 8 minutes.

To make chips, slice the tortillas into 6 wedges. (Leave the tortillas whole if you're making tostadas.) Cover a large swath of countertop with clean brown paper bags, newspaper, kitchen towels, or paper towels for draining.

To make chips, add about 10 tortilla pieces to the pan, one at a time, being careful not to crowd them (or else they will stick to one another). Fry each batch for 2 minutes: they will begin to puff and curl slightly and their bubbling will cease. Flip the chips (ideally, with tongs; if not, use 2 utensils) and fry for an additional 1 to 2 minutes on the second side, depending on the thickness of your tortillas. Adjust the heat as necessary to keep the chips from burning. The finished chips should be golden and crisp throughout.

Remove the chips with tongs or a slotted spoon into a small sieve or wire basket held over the pan, and let them drain for a moment to leave behind as much oil as possible.

Transfer the chips to the paper in a single layer, not touching, to drain, and salt to taste. Let them cool for about 3 minutes—they will crisp up as they cool—and devour while still warm. Discard (or eat!) any chips that did not crisp up all the way through.

To make tostadas, fry the whole tortillas, one at a time, as above for about 2 minutes per side, until golden and crispy throughout, pressing down on them slightly from time to time as they fry. Drain well, letting excess oil drip into the pan from the fried tortilla, then transfer it to the paper-lined countertop.

HOW TO STORE IT Fully cooled chips can be stored in an airtight container or zip-top bag for up to 1 week.

PLUS: simple salsa Makes about 1 1/2 cups

INSTRUCTIONS Need a little salsa with that? Combine the following in a bowl: 1 1/2 cups chopped tomato (about 1 large tomato); 3 tablespoons chopped green onion, white and green parts; 1/4 cup packed cilantro leaves; 1/2 teaspoon kosher salt; 1 1/2 tablespoons fresh lime juice or white wine vinegar. Serve promptly.

tamales (two ways)

Makes about 20 tamales
(if using masa harina)
or 30 tamales (if using
fresh masa)

TIME COMMITMENT
about 1 day

Peeling back a fresh, hot tamale is like opening up a present on Christmas morning. There's no point, IMHO, in making just a few: if you're going to make tamales, then by all means grab multiple corn husks with mucho gusto and go. In addition to their innate deliciousness and crowd-pleasingness, they freeze into the best fast food ever. If you've got your own homemade masa on hand (see page 62), all the better. If not, you can take a shortcut with store-bought masa harina. While tamale steamers will certainly do the job, placing a rack over a baking sheet steams more tamales in less time and does not require any special equipment. Oh, and dried corn husks are available in Latin American grocery stores or online.

1 (1 1/2-ounce) package dried corn husks

1 cup vegetable shortening or lard

1 tablespoon kosher salt

1 or 2 teaspoons baking powder

3 cups masa harina, or 2 1/2 pounds fresh masa (page 62)

2 cups water (if using masa harina)

1 3/4 to 3 cups tamale filling (see page 71)

INSTRUCTIONS Put the corn husks in a large bowl, add water to cover the husks by at least 1 inch, and soak for 4 hours or overnight.

Make the tamale dough. Using an electric beater or a stand mixer, cream the shortening until it's quite white and fluffy; about 5 minutes. Add the salt and baking powder to the shortening (use 1 teaspoon of baking powder if you're using masa harina; use 2 teaspoons if you're using fresh masa) and beat to combine thoroughly.

If you're making tamales with masa harina, combine the masa harina in a bowl with 2 cups of water and stir well to form a coarse, crumbly dough.

Beat the masa harina dough, or the fresh masa, if you're using that, into the shortening in 3 parts, scraping down the sides of the bowl between each addition.

Now, roll the tamales. If you made masa harina tamale dough, you'll need 1 3/4 cups of filling, and you'll be making about 20 tamales. If you're using fresh masa, you'll need 3 cups of filling, and you'll be making about 30 tamales. You will have plenty of corn husks left over; compost the odd pieces and any other unused husks.

Lay a clean, dry kitchen towel on a work surface. Make certain that the corn husks for rolling have been soaking in water for at least 4 hours. Find 1 whole, untorn husk and pair it up with another whole, untorn husk, or piece together 3 or 4 smaller pieces of husk. Make sure the husks are free of grit and corn silk; run them under tap water if you need to. Lay the husks flat in an overlapping position on the towel: you want the working surface area to be about 3 inches across by 2 inches tall, and the husks

// CONTINUED

should overlap by about 1 inch. Dry the tops of the husks gently with a kitchen towel.

With wet fingertips, scoop up about 1/4 cup of tamale dough and pat it down in the center of the husks in a rectangular shape about the size of a playing card. Spoon 1 rounded tablespoonful of filling just north of the center of the dough.

Roll the half of the husk that's closest to you toward the top, letting the dough cover the filling. Fold the left side and then the right side of the husk in toward the center, and then roll it one more time away from you, ensuring that the seam of the husk is on the bottom. If you're making more than one kind of tamale, mark the outside of the husk with its contents using a marker. The tamale should be well folded with the husks tucked snugly in place; if not, use kitchen string, strips of corn husk, or unwaxed, unflavored dental floss to tie the husks in place.

To steam the tamales, preheat the oven to 350°F.

Place 2 rimmed baking sheets or large baking dishes near the oven. Pour enough water into each pan to cover the bottom and place an ovenproof wire rack on or in each pan. Place rolled tamales on each rack in a single layer, seam side down: it's okay if they touch one another. Cover the racks very tightly with heavy-duty aluminum foil, using multiple sheets if necessary to make a tight seal with the edges of the pans. If your rack is much larger than the pan, start by placing one or more extra-long sheets of foil underneath the dish (do this before you add the water to the dish) and bring the ends up over the tamale-filled racks, folding the foil to make a tight seal. Carefully place both trays of tamales in the oven and steam for 1 hour.

Be very careful when removing the foil from your tamales! It is very hot and steamy inside the foil, and the steam and hot water in the pans can burn you. Feel free to let the tamales sit in the steam tent for up to an hour before you're ready to serve. Your tamales are ready to eat immediately—eat them hot.

HOW TO STORE IT Let the tamales cool at room temperature, then transfer to an airtight container and refrigerate for up to 1 week. Frozen airtight and wrapped individually in plastic, they will last for up to 6 months. To eat, either re-steam or heat refrigerated or frozen tamales in the microwave, still in the husk, plastic wrap removed, for 2 to 3 minutes, until hot.

PLUS: fillings for tamales

Make sure your tamale fillings are cool enough to handle before using them. Note that leftover tamale filling can make a great lunch served over rice or atop a tostada.

CHICKEN PICADILLO

Makes about 3 cups (enough to fill about 30 tamales)

2 tablespoons neutral vegetable oil
1 yellow onion, finely chopped
Kosher salt
3 cloves garlic, minced
1 pound skinless, boneless chicken, finely chopped
1/4 cup raisins, finely chopped
1/4 cup finely chopped black olives
3 tablespoons capers
1/4 teaspoon ground cinnamon
Juice of 1/2 lime
Black pepper

INSTRUCTIONS Heat the oil in a skillet over medium-high heat and sauté the onion with a pinch of salt until it starts to brown around the edges, about 8 minutes. Add the garlic and sauté for 1 minute more. Add the chicken and sauté until it's cooked through, about 5 minutes. Turn down the heat to medium and add the raisins, olives, capers, and cinnamon. Stir well to combine and sauté for another 3 to 4 minutes, until heated thoroughly and fragrant. Turn off the heat and add the lime juice, plus salt and pepper to taste.

HOW TO STORE IT Refrigerated, this will keep for up to 1 week.

BEAN AND CHEESE TAMALE FILLING

Makes about 31/2 cups (enough to fill about 40 tamales)

1 cup dried pinto beans
3 tablespoons vegetable oil
1 yellow onion, chopped
5 cloves garlic, thinly sliced
2 bay leaves
1 cup chopped green onions (about 6 onions, tough green parts removed)
8 ounces Cheddar cheese, grated
Kosher salt and black pepper

INSTRUCTIONS Cover the beans in cool water by at least one inch. Let them soak overnight, or for at least 6 hours.

Drain the soaked beans completely and rinse them well in a colander. Put a large pot over medium heat, add the oil, and cook the onion until soft, about 5 minutes. Stir in the garlic and cook for about 1 minute, until fragrant. Pour the beans into the pot and add the bay leaves and just enough water to cover the beans. Bring to a boil over high heat and immediately lower the heat to a slow simmer. Cover and cook for 50 to 60 minutes, or until tender, stirring occasionally. Drain the beans and discard the bay leaves. Transfer the beans to a bowl and toss with the green onions and cheese, adding salt and pepper to taste.

HOW TO STORE IT The filling can be kept refrigerated for up to 5 days or frozen for up to 3 months.

7 | roast it

Roasting just about anything is probably the best way I can think of to perfume the entire house. The art of roasting is not limited to chicken and potatoes. It's also the basis for dozens of quirky culinary projects—coffee beans, cacao nibs, nuts, and chestnuts, to name a few.

The trick with some of the projects in this chapter is often just in finding the raw materials to work with: I'll give you tips on procurement when necessary. Once your materials are in hand, however, you'll find the process of home roasting to be meditative and entirely enjoyable. And, of course, the results of your thoughtful labor will be roasty-toasty pleasure.

coffee beans

Makes 7 ounces

TIME COMMITMENT
about 20 minutes

If you are serious about/obsessed with roasting your own coffee, numerous manufacturers are standing by to take your money for hardcore roasting machinery. Also—much like bong building—coffee roasting seems to lend itself to home hardware hobbyists: look no further than your local laptop to find people hacking popcorn makers and more ("Dude, let me show you my new vacuum cleaner–powered coffee roaster. It's AWESOME!"). For those of you who just want to test the waters and keep it simple, I am happy to report that you need nothing more than a heavy pan, green coffee beans, and a wooden spoon. Oh, and an exhaust fan: coffee is a spitting, steam-producing dragon in the kitchen, and good ventilation is an absolute must. If you can't find green beans at your local health food store, buy them online from SweetMarias.com, CoffeeStoreHouse.com, or a host of other retailers.

8 ounces green coffee beans

INSTRUCTIONS Place a large metal bowl in the freezer to chill. Activate your kitchen's best ventilation: open windows and doors, turn on fans—whatever you have. This is a must!

I recommend using an uncovered Dutch oven with a heavy bottom for roasting your beans: the high sides will help reduce the mess from the popping coffee hulls. However, if you don't have one, a cast-iron or other heavy skillet will suffice.

Place the beans in the cold pan, put the pan over medium heat, and start stirring with a sturdy wooden spoon. You will need to stir constantly throughout the entire roasting process: you are trying to keep the heat as even as possible among all of the beans throughout the roast.

After about 5 minutes, the beans will begin to crack and smoke. About 10 minutes more, and the beans will be

// CONTINUED

coffee beans, CONTINUED

turning chestnut in color: a very light roast. Ten to fifteen minutes beyond that (30 minutes total), and you'll have a dark, nearly black roast. If you like a medium roast, you'll stop somewhere in the middle. Note that you need to take the beans off the heat a little bit before they turn the color you like: they will continue to roast a little after you stop the cooking process.

Once the beans are just a shade lighter than the color you desire, take them off the heat. They will continue to color slightly until you pour them into the chilled bowl and stir constantly for about 3 minutes. Rotate the bowl to cool down the beans quickly and evenly. Then pour the beans into a colander, place the colander over the bowl, and stir for another minute or so to sift out the flyaway hulls.

Your coffee is ready to be ground and brewed as usual, though it will be much better if you wait until the next day to grind it.

HOW TO STORE IT The roasted, cooled whole beans can be stored in an airtight container at room temperature, and the coffee will be at its best, for up to 2 weeks.

sweet and spicy nuts

Makes about 2 cups

TIME COMMITMENT
about 1 hour

Snackmasters, prepare to feed your food hole. These addictive nuts have every taste sensation you're craving: from heat to sweet to salt to fat. And since they're nuts, you can sort of pretend that they're actually kind of good for you. Needless to say, a gift of these in a fancy stenciled vessel or served to your cocktail-drinking guests by the handful will be most appreciated. This is also a good way to breathe new life into older nuts that may be on their way to staleness.

1 tablespoon butter

1 tablespoon neutral vegetable oil

$1/2$ teaspoon cayenne pepper

3 tablespoons brown sugar

1 teaspoon dried rosemary

1 teaspoon kosher salt

2 cups almonds, cashews, pecans, walnuts, or peanuts, or a combination

INSTRUCTIONS Line a baking sheet with parchment paper and set aside. Melt the butter and the oil in a skillet over medium heat. Add the cayenne, sugar, rosemary, and salt and stir for 30 seconds. Add the nuts to the pan and toss to coat. Toast for about 8 minutes, until the nuts brown, stirring constantly to keep them from burning.

Transfer the nuts to the prepared baking sheet and let them cool completely.

HOW TO STORE IT Stored in an airtight container at room temperature, these will keep for up to 1 month.

cacao nibs

Makes about 6 ounces
(about 2 cups)

TIME COMMITMENT
less than 2 hours

Chocolate chips, you've been kicked to the curb. Just get yourselves out of my cookies right now. There's a new sheriff in town named cacao nibs, and they are my preferred baking companions across the board. These precursors to chocolate are chocolaty without being sweet, packed with toothsome texture and übernuttiness. They are roasted similarly to coffee, but prepped the way you would fava beans—peeling one bean at a time. (I can get it done in a single one-hour episode of *Top Chef*.) If you can't find raw cacao beans in your health food store's bulk foods section, you can order them online.

8 ounces (about 1 3/4 cups) raw cacao beans

INSTRUCTIONS Place a large metal bowl in the freezer to chill.

Place the beans in a cold, heavy skillet or Dutch oven, put the pan over medium heat, and start stirring with a sturdy wooden spoon. You will need to stir constantly throughout the entire roasting process: you are trying to keep the heat even. Roast for about 10 minutes for a medium roast, and 13 minutes for a darker roast. You will hear some very loud cracks and pops from your beans: this is a normal—if alarming—part of the process. Note that there won't be a lot of visual change to the beans, but they will become fragrant as they cook.

Once the beans are roasted to your satisfaction, take the bowl from the freezer and pour in the beans quickly to stop the roasting. Stir constantly, rotating the bowl, for about 3 minutes, to help the beans cool quickly.

Once they're cool enough to handle, each bean must be peeled to remove the thin bark from the outside. Rub the bean between your fingers, and its papery husk will slide off easily, but be careful not to crush the bean. Discard the husks: the dark shiny interior bean is your cacao.

Once all beans have been shelled, a quick pulse in the food processor (or a gentle hammering in a plastic bag) will chop them to small pieces (nibs). Use them in baking whenever you would chocolate chips.

HOW TO STORE IT Kept airtight at room temperature, cacao nibs will last for up to 4 months.

PLUS: cacao nib brittle

Want to enjoy your nibs immediately? Try this brittle.

INSTRUCTIONS Line a rimmed baking sheet with parchment paper and set aside. In a small saucepan, combine 1 cup water, 1/2 cup sugar, and 1/2 cup chopped cacao nibs and bring to a boil over high heat, uncovered. Stir often until the nibs begin to melt and turn the liquid chocolate brown, about 12 minutes. Pour the hot liquid onto the prepared baking sheet and let cool completely, about 25 minutes. Once the brittle is cool, shatter it into small pieces. Wrapped in wax paper or parchment paper in an airtight container, this will last for 1 week.

roasted chestnuts

Makes about 12 ounces
(about 2 cups)

TIME COMMITMENT
about 3 hours

If you've never had the pleasure of picking apart a freshly roasted chestnut hot from the oven on a chilly day, then you owe your fingers an apology. Peel back the hard outer shell and slough off the inner papery husk, and within is a tender, delicate, chewy, flavorful nutmeat that's entirely worth your effort. In my house, these are devoured fresh from the oven while we're standing at the kitchen counter. If you can restrain yourself, use them for a classic Thanksgiving chestnut stuffing or soup.

1 pound fresh chestnuts

INSTRUCTIONS Lay one chestnut down on its flat side on a cutting board. Using a sharp serrated knife, cut a deep X into the rounded side of the nut. Note that you should not cut all the way through the chestnut, but your cut should be just deep enough to pierce both the outer shell and the husk underneath it. Follow suit with the remainder of the chestnuts.

Transfer the chestnuts to a bowl and cover with water by 1 inch. Let them sit for 1 hour. Approximately 15 minutes before that hour is up, preheat the oven to 400°F.

Drain the chestnuts and arrange them on a rimmed baking sheet in a single layer, X-cut side up. Roast for 25 minutes, until the cut corners of the shells begin to curl up and the exposed nut beneath is beginning to turn brown.

As soon as the chestnuts are cool enough to handle, they are ready to be peeled and eaten.

HOW TO STORE IT Once they are completely cool, they will keep, stored airtight at room temperature, for up to 5 days.

8 | hunt it

Meat is a glorious thing, my omnivore friends. Meat on a stick? Pure perfection. Homemade deli meats between two slabs of rye? A thing of utter beauty. This chapter is designed to fulfill all of your meat-filled dreams.

The Jewish deli staples of corned beef and pastrami are the stuff of crowd-pleasing, make-ahead sandwich extravaganzas. And your barbecue guests will be truly dazzled when you offer them handmade weenies, whether deep-fried in a cornmeal crust or hot off the grill. For extra credit, I encourage you to pair them with your own handmade buns (page 55).

I love offering frozen tinfoil-wrapped packages with a band of pretty paper for birthdays and the holidays. I promise you that a gift of well-salted, well-cured flesh will be one gift that will not be returned.

Grab your hunting stick: we're in hot pursuit of real meaty flavor.

corned beef

Makes 3 to 3 1/2 pounds

TIME COMMITMENT
about 5 days

"Corning" meat is another term for a long, slow brining process—and it's delicious both hot (with potatoes, cabbage, and beer) and sliced cold for sandwiches (don't forget the mustard). Any meat that will sit in the fridge uncooked for a week should have a dousing of Instacure #1, the pink curing salt (known as sodium nitrite) available at some butcher shops or at SausageMaker.com. Not only will curing salt help prevent dietary cooties, but it will also help the beef keep its delightful color.

3/4 cup kosher salt

3/4 cup sugar

6 cups water, plus more as needed

2 teaspoons Instacure #1

1 large bay leaf

2 teaspoons brown mustard seed

2 teaspoons celery seed

1 teaspoon caraway

4 cloves garlic, crushed

1 tablespoon black peppercorns

2 star anise

4 pounds well-marbled ("first cut") beef brisket

4 new potatoes, cut into cubes (optional)

3 large carrots, peeled and cut into large chunks (optional)

1/2 head cabbage, cut in half, core intact (optional)

INSTRUCTIONS In a container large enough to hold all of the liquid and the meat, stir the salt and the sugar into the 6 cups of water to dissolve; the solution will be cloudy. Add the Instacure #1, bay, mustard seed, celery seed, caraway, garlic, peppercorns, and anise, and stir. Put the meat in the brine, making sure it is completely submerged: add more water as necessary to cover. An inverted plate on top of the meat can help push it down into the liquid. Cover with a sealed lid or plastic wrap and let the beef rest in the refrigerator for 5 days, stirring on day 3 to redistribute the spices. The beef will be fully cured when it feels stiff and resilient when poked; it should have the firmness of very well-done meat throughout.

Once the meat is cured, drain it, and discard the brine and all the solid ingredients. Place the meat in a large stockpot and cover with fresh water by 1 inch. Cover and bring to a boil over high heat, then reduce the heat to medium and simmer, covered, for 1 1/2 hours. If you're making a meal out of this, add the potatoes, carrots, and cabbage to the pot after an hour. The meat's internal temperature must be 150°F.

To serve, remove the meat from the pot with tongs, draining off as much liquid as you can. Trim away large hunks of excess fat and slice the meat against the grain and on a bias. Plate a few slices along with the potatoes, carrots, and cabbage. For sandwiches, serve the meat hot or cold and sliced as thinly as possible.

HOW TO STORE IT Refrigerated, corned beef will keep for up to 1 week. It can also be wrapped tightly and frozen for up to 4 months.

pastrami

Makes 3 to 3 1/2 pounds

TIME COMMITMENT
about 5 days

Jewish bacon, anyone? You may or may not already know that pastrami is just corned beef that has been smoked, rather than boiled, and that the flavor difference between the two is mile high. Please note that while your pastrami will be ready to eat fresh from the grill, its initial saltiness will really bowl you over. It truly takes a day for the flavors to meld properly. Aside from that, the only trick here is in getting the slices really thin. To do so more easily, freeze your finished, cooled pastrami for about 20 minutes to firm it up, then go at it with your sharpest knife. If you're using a gas grill rather than charcoal, I suggest using some hickory sawdust to add to the smoke flavor (I get mine from SausageMaker.com).

3 to 3 1/2 pounds Corned Beef (page 82), fully cured and drained but not boiled

2 teaspoons finely crushed black peppercorns

INSTRUCTIONS Rinse the beef well and pat it dry. Place it on a rack over a dish or plate and refrigerate, uncovered, for 30 minutes (while the charcoal heats). The goal here is to allow as much air flow as possible to help the surface of the meat dry and absorb smoke better.

Meanwhile, light enough real hardwood charcoal to fill half of a charcoal starter chimney. After 20 to 30 minutes, the coals will be profoundly white from heat and the flames will have completely died down.

Rake the coals to one side of the barbecue grill and open up the grill's vents underneath.

If you're using a gas grill, heat one side of the grill to low heat. Scoop 3 cups of hickory sawdust into the middle of a large sheet of aluminum foil. Wrap the foil around the sawdust as if you were wrapping a present; the result should be a flat, square pack. Flip it over, and using the tip of a knife, stab about 15 small holes into the package to allow smoke from the sawdust to escape. Place the foil

pack, holes side up, directly onto the grill's lava rocks or grill plate.

A few minutes before the grill is ready, take the meat out of the refrigerator and rub the crushed pepper all over its surface. Make sure the grill grate is clean, and place the meat on the "cool" side of the grill (the side without coals), with the thickest part of the meat closest to the coals and the fattiest side up. Cover the grill and position the vents over the meat.

Smoke the meat for 2 to 2 1/2 hours, until its internal temperature reaches 150°F. If you're using a charcoal grill, you may need to light more coals after 1 to 1 1/2 hours of cooking time; if the grill lid feels hot and at least a slight trickle of smoke is piping out from the top vents, the coals are still hot enough.

Allow the meat to cool completely, wrap it in foil, and then refrigerate for 1 day before eating.

HOW TO STORE IT Well-wrapped, it can stay refrigerated for up to 1 week. Frozen, wrapped in foil twice and sealed in a zip-top bag, the pastrami will keep for up to 4 months. Refrigerate for 24 hours to thaw.

hot dogs

Makes about fifteen
6-inch hot dogs

TIME COMMITMENT
about 4 1/2 hours

Hot dogs? HOT DOG! Once upon a time, these and other sausages were frightening tubular vessels for all of the leftovers and scraps of the butcher shop. But if you're diggin' in on your own dogs, you can use the same good-quality meat that you would serve for supper. I debated the pork/beef dichotomy of the dog, but I eventually settled on beef only. Here's why: hot dogs are an emulsified sausage, meaning that all of the meat and fat have to come together into one solid suspension to create the right smooth texture (think about putting together a mayonnaise). This means keeping your meat "batter" very cold at all times—a tricky thing for the home cook, and beef is more forgiving. It also means no hot appliances for the stuffing, so forget your KitchenAid and use a cake decorating kit instead. If you can't find sausage casings and Instacure locally, buy them online at SausageMaker.com (though note that, here, the Instacure is optional: it's just used for color).

2 pounds ground chuck

4 (3-foot) pieces 3/4-inch natural sausage casing
(22–24 mm sheep casing)

4 cloves garlic

2 eggs

2 tablespoons sweet paprika

2 tablespoons prepared yellow mustard

1 teaspoon ground white pepper

2 teaspoons sugar

2 tablespoons kosher salt

1/4 teaspoon Instacure #1 (optional)

8 ice cubes, plus more for the water bath

4 tablespoons vegetable oil

INSTRUCTIONS If you're grinding your own beef, do so the day before and make certain it chills for 24 hours.

Fill a small bowl with water and put the sausage casings in to soak for at least 30 minutes while you put the hot dogs together. Place a bowl (preferably metal) large enough to hold the meat in the refrigerator to cool.

We're going to grind the hot dog forcemeat in two batches. For batch number one, finely mince 2 cloves of the garlic in a food processor fitted with the steel blade. Add 1 egg, and half each of the paprika, mustard, pepper, sugar, salt, and Instacure, if using. Blend well.

Add 2 ice cubes to the food processor and crush them with the spices, about 40 seconds. Then, add 1 pound of the very cold meat and grind it until it is a fine paste and the spices are incorporated, about 60 seconds. Turn off

// CONTINUED

the motor and nestle 2 more ice cubes into the meat mixture. Process to crush the ice for another 40 to 60 seconds; when it is sufficiently ground, the meat will be a smooth paste. With the machine running, drizzle in 2 tablespoons of the oil and let it mix in entirely, about 20 seconds. Using a rubber spatula to scrape it out of the bowl of the food processor, transfer this batch of forcemeat to the chilled bowl and put it in the refrigerator to keep cold.

Grind the second batch of meat and spices the same way. Scrape it into the bowl with the other forcemeat, return to the refrigerator, and let chill for 30 minutes.

Meanwhile, wash the casings. Drain off their soaking water, then take 1 piece of casing and affix one end to the nozzle of your kitchen faucet (or if it can't fit your faucet, a funnel). Turn on the water and allow it to run through the casing, using your hands to help guide the water out the other end. Flush the casing out completely for about 1 minute. Repeat with the remaining pieces of casing. Return the cleaned casings to the bowl and cover with fresh water.

Now, fashion a double ice bath. Find two mixing bowls—one large one to hold an ice bath, and one small enough to fit inside it that can hold at least half the meat. When you are nearly ready to start stuffing, fill the bottom bowl about 1/3 full with ice and water and place the smaller bowl in the ice bath to chill completely.

Ready your hand stuffer (if you have one) or fit a sturdy pastry bag with a long tip and a wide hole. Take 1 casing from the bowl and slide one end onto the nozzle of the hand stuffer or onto the pastry tip. Continue to slide the length of the casing onto the nozzle or tip, leaving a tail of about 2 inches.

Spoon 1/3 of the forcemeat into the cold bowl above the ice bath (keep the rest in the refrigerator), being careful not to allow any of the ice water to seep into the bowl with the meat. Now fill the hand stuffer or pastry bag with the forcemeat and fold down the top of the bag. Holding on to the casing, start squeezing hard enough to force the meat through the tip and into the casing. A lot of air will be squeezed out at first. Joke about it. Let that pass and then, once the meat is coming out in full force, tie a snug knot in the casing right up against the edge of the meat. You will get the hang of this.

Keep squeezing, trying to fill the casing firmly but not too snugly—it's up to you how plump you want your hot dogs to be, but they should at minimum feel solid and hold their shape. Keep filling the pastry bag and then the casing with meat until you have at least a 2-inch tail of unused casing on the finishing end. Knot the tail next to the meat tightly.

To make individual hot dogs, twist sections into the long dog you've just created. A 6-inch segment will fit a standard bun. Twist the first dog into shape simply by twisting the casing about 5 turns. To make subsequent dogs, be sure to twist in the opposite direction (for example, if you started by twisting the casing clockwise, twist counterclockwise the second time, clockwise the third time, and so on). You will end up with a string of links—just like in old cartoons. Coil in a single layer, not touching, on a rimmed baking sheet and move to the refrigerator; keep uncovered.

Continue the stuffing process with a new casing and keep stuffing until you run out of meat. Make certain that your meat remains cold while you work, moving it in batches from the refrigerator to the ice bath and adding ice to the bath as necessary. Discard any unused casings.

Allow your finished hot dogs to set up in the fridge, for at least 1 hour and up to 24.

To cook, bring a large pot of water to a boil and then turn down the heat until the water stops boiling. Add the hot dogs to the pot, cover, and let them sit in the very hot water (not boiling!) until they reach 150°F inside, about 15 minutes, depending on their size. At this point, your hot dogs are ready to eat or store. Cooked hot dogs can be reheated in warm water, about 12 minutes. But grilling or pan searing them will yield the best flavor.

HOW TO STORE IT Wrapped tightly, they will keep refrigerated for 1 week or frozen for 4 months. Separate finished dogs from one another by simply snipping them apart with kitchen shears.

corn dogs

Makes 6 corn dogs

TIME COMMITMENT
about 45 minutes

Mmmmm . . . carnival food. After eating these things, I recommend a few trips on the Tilt-A-Whirl, followed by a couple paper plates of elephant ears. But seriously, food on a stick always tastes better, right? And I assure you these will not disappoint. And while we are quick to file this under the header "junk food," if you start with your own wholesome homemade hot dogs (page 85) or nonmeat pups, and fry properly in fresh oil, these aren't really so naughty after all. The only trick lies in proper frying technique: make sure your oil is the right temperature, and be sure to size up your dogs-on-sticks against your wok before you start cooking to make certain that they will be able to lie flat in the oil. Do not use elongated hot dogs: nothing larger than the standard-issue seven inches. (Insert joke here.)

1/2 cup masa harina

1/4 cup plus 1 tablespoon all-purpose flour, plus more for dusting

1 tablespoon sugar

1/2 teaspoon kosher salt

Pinch of finely ground black pepper

1 egg

3/4 cup milk

6 (7-inch or smaller) hot dogs, homemade (page 85) or store-bought

6 long wooden barbecue skewers

6 cups neutral vegetable oil

INSTRUCTIONS In a very large bowl with a wide bottom, combine the masa harina, flour, sugar, salt, and pepper and whisk together. Crack the egg in a separate cup or bowl, beat it lightly, and add it to the flour mixture, along with the milk. Stir with a fork or whisk until smooth. Set this batter aside to rest.

While the batter is resting, blot the hot dogs with paper towels to get them as dry as possible. Insert skewers into the tops of the hot dogs lengthwise, pushing the skewer about halfway through. Sprinkle the skewered dogs with a thin coating of flour (this will help the batter adhere) and rub the flour over the surface of each hot dog evenly.

Set up a cooling rack covered with paper towels, and pour the oil into a large wok; it should be at least 1 1/2 inches deep. Heat the oil over medium-high to high heat for 8 to 10 minutes, until it is shimmering and just beginning to smoke. You may also test the oil's readiness by dropping in a teaspoon of batter. It will fry to golden brown in about 20 seconds. (Remove it from the oil with a slotted spoon.)

Have a sturdy set of tongs standing by. Dip a single dog completely into the batter (you may need to use a spoon to coat it all the way up to the stick), twirl to let the excess drip off, and then gently place the dog in the oil. It's a good idea to keep the stick out of the oil as much as possible, but it's okay if some of it dips in. The total frying time will be 1 to 2 minutes, but you will need to gently turn the corn dog a couple of times with the tongs to fry it evenly on all sides. Fry one corn dog at a time, pulling them from the oil when they're golden brown.

Transfer the corn dogs to the cooling rack for about 2 minutes, then serve right away.

HOW TO STORE IT Wrapped airtight, these will keep refrigerated for 1 week or frozen for up to 4 months. To reheat, bake on a rack in the toaster oven set at 325°F for about 10 minutes.

9 | smoke it

If grilled food is a well-crowned beauty queen, smoked food is its more bookish, turtleneck-wearing, down-to-earth cousin. When the majesty of big flames dies down, a low, slow fire adds serious flavor—to meats, yes, but also, surprisingly and seductively, to the earthy flavor of nuts and the sweetness of fall fruits.

And a little bit of smoke goes a long way. A dollop of smoky hot sauce gives meat true sizzle. And smoked nuts, cheese, or fruit bring leagues of depth to a salad or a compote. In this chapter, we tackle the art of hot-smoking, and some of the glorious ingredients that it can create.

chipotles in adobo sauce

Makes about 6 cups

TIME COMMITMENT
about 4 hours

I'm a huge fan of the smoky heat of this double-duty condiment: pop the lid and you have both fiery smoked jalapeños and the flavor-power sauce in which they have been floating. For years, I relied on canned *chipotles en adobo*, but I've done my best to replicate those flavors in a from-scratch version, and I'm really happy with the results. Both chiles and sauce grace my table in every form—on chicken, omelets, tacos, and burritos, and even in Indian curries. If you're using a gas grill rather than charcoal, I suggest using some hickory sawdust to add to the smoke flavor (I get mine from SausageMaker.com).

1 pound red jalapeño or red Fresno chiles

1 1/2 cups coarsely chopped tomato

1 3/4 cups coarsely chopped onion

2 cloves garlic

2 teaspoons dried oregano

2 tablespoons sugar

1/2 cup plus 1 tablespoon distilled white vinegar

1 tablespoon kosher salt

6 tablespoons tomato paste

INSTRUCTIONS First, we'll smoke the peppers. Wash them and dry them; leave the stems intact.

Open the top and bottom vents of a barbecue grill and light a moderate amount of mesquite hardwood coals; enough to fill a chimney starter about halfway. In 20 to 30 minutes, the flames in the coals will have died down and they will be glowing and turning white. Pour the coals into one side of the grill: we want to get the chiles to smoke from indirect heat and not roast from high, direct heat. If you're using a gas grill, heat one side of the grill to low heat. Scoop 3 cups of hickory sawdust into the middle of a large sheet of aluminum foil. Wrap the foil around

the sawdust as if you were wrapping a present; the result should be a flat, square pack. Flip it over, and using the tip of a knife, stab about 15 small holes into the package to allow smoke from the sawdust to escape. Place the foil pack, holes side up, directly onto the grill's lava rocks or grill plate.

Place the chiles in a single layer on the "cool" side of the grill. Cover the grill, positioning the open vents over the chiles. The entire smoking process will take about 1 1/2 hours; the chiles should be rotated and turned about halfway through. The chiles will be finished smoking when they smell of smoke and they have softened somewhat, with a small amount of char in spots. At this point, the chiles can sit for up to 3 days, covered and refrigerated.

Now we'll make the sauce. In a blender, combine the tomato, onion, garlic, oregano, sugar, vinegar, salt, and tomato paste and blend until smooth. Scrape the sauce into a small covered saucepan, add the chiles, and bring to a boil over medium-high heat (note that while there isn't a tremendous amount of sauce, it should be just enough to

// CONTINUED

chipotles in adobo sauce, CONTINUED

cover the fruit). Reduce the heat to low, cover, and keep on a very low simmer, stirring occasionally, for 60 to 75 minutes. The chiles should soften further but not burst, and the sauce will take on a darker hue.

HOW TO STORE IT When they're cool enough to handle, pour chiles and sauce into 2 or 3 glass jars, seal tightly, and refrigerate for up to 2 months.

smoked almonds

Makes 2 cups

TIME COMMITMENT
about 1 1/2 hours

Freshly roasted nuts are good, but freshly smoked nuts are an unexpected hit parade. This recipe offers a lot of flexibility. You can either smoke 'em raw or add new life to stale preroasted or even previously flavored nuts. The smoke here is subtle but substantial, and these make a great homespun giftie. If almonds aren't your thing, this also works well with hazelnuts and peanuts, but not so swell with pecans and walnuts. Note that the perforated aluminum pan can be reused. If you're using a gas grill rather than charcoal, I suggest using some hickory sawdust to add to the smoke flavor (I get mine from SausageMaker.com).

2 cups roasted or raw almonds, salted or unsalted

INSTRUCTIONS Open the top and bottom vents of a barbecue grill and light a moderate amount of mesquite hardwood coals; enough to fill a chimney starter about halfway. In 20 to 30 minutes, the flames in the coals will have died down and they will be glowing and turning white. Pour the coals into one side of the grill: we want the nuts to smoke over indirect heat, not roast or burn over direct heat. If you're using a gas grill, heat one side of the grill to low heat. Scoop 3 cups of hickory sawdust into the middle of a large sheet of aluminum foil. Wrap the foil around the sawdust as if you were wrapping a present; the result should be a flat, square pack. Flip it over, and using the tip of a knife, stab about 15 small holes into the package to allow smoke from the sawdust to escape. Place the foil pack, holes side up, directly onto the grill's lava rocks or grill plate.

For the nuts, flip over an 8-inch square disposable aluminum pan so that its bottom is facing up. Using a sharp knife, cut a couple dozen slits into the bottom and sides of the pan. These will let smoke pass through the pan and around the nuts. Pour the nuts into the pan and shake them into a single layer. Place the nuts on the "cool" side of the grill, away from the coals or grill plate. Cover the grill, positioning the open vents over the nuts.

Smoke the almonds for 1 hour, shaking or stirring the pan halfway through. Use caution, as the aluminum pan will be hot.

Remove the pan from the grill and pour the nuts into a serving bowl; serve immediately.

HOW TO STORE IT Let the nuts cool and seal them in an airtight jar; they'll remain delicious for up to 2 months in the pantry.

smoked apples and pears

Makes about 11 ounces

TIME COMMITMENT
about 2 hours

Smoked fruit is just wicked—a totally unique set of flavors. Try it! What can you do with smoked fruit in your kitchen? It adds another dimension to a chicken sandwich or a salad; it can be pureed into an apple or pear butter or chopped into an apple-Cheddar pie; it can be added to a cheese plate. I recommend using fruit that's ripe but very firm. The hickory sawdust called for in this recipe can be found at SausageMaker.com.

1 large sweet apple
1 large ripe but firm pear
1 teaspoon kosher salt
2 teaspoons fresh lemon juice

INSTRUCTIONS Tear off a large sheet of heavy-duty aluminum foil. In the center of the foil, scoop 2 cups of hickory sawdust, then fold the foil into a flat packet. Flip the foil pack over and cut a dozen small slits into the foil: this will allow the smoke from the hickory to escape and smoke the fruit.

Open the top and bottom vents of a barbecue grill and light a moderate amount of mesquite hardwood coals: enough to fill a chimney starter halfway. In 20 to 30 minutes, the flames on the coals will have died down and they will be glowing and turning white. Pour the coals into one side of the grill: we want the fruit to smoke over indirect heat, not grill over high, direct heat. Lay the foil packet of sawdust, holey side up, on top of the coals. Put the grill's top rack into place.

If you're using a gas grill, heat one side of the grill to low heat, and put the prepared foil pack of sawdust directly onto the grill's lava rocks or grill plate.

Meanwhile, slice the apple and pear into 8 half-moon pieces each, discarding the cores but leaving the skins intact. In a small bowl, toss the fruit slices with the salt and the lemon juice.

Flip over an 8-inch square disposable aluminum pan so that its bottom is facing up. Using a sharp knife, cut a couple dozen slits into the bottom and sides of the pan. These will let smoke pass through the pan and around the fruit. Arrange the fruit slices in the pan, skin side down and in a single layer, not touching. Place the pan on the "cool" side of the grill, away from the coals or grill plate. Cover the grill and position the open vents over the fruit.

Smoke the fruit for 1 1/2 hours, rotating the pan 180 degrees halfway through. Use caution, as the aluminum pan will be hot.

Take the pan from the heat and transfer the fruit to another container—it's ready to eat or use immediately.

HOW TO STORE IT Kept in an airtight container in the fridge, the fruit will remain delicious for 10 days. The flavor is greatly improved if the fruit is allowed to come to room temperature again before serving.

smoked cheese

Makes about 7 1/2 ounces

TIME COMMITMENT
about 1 1/2 hours

Far be it from me to stick a pin in your cheese-smoking dreams, but we have to set some ground rules from the get-go. We will be hot-smoking cheese on a barbecue grill; therefore, the cheese varieties we can use are indeed a closed set. The smoked Cheddars of the world are cold-smoked, a process that involves way more hardware and backyard space than I can even wrap my brain around. Experiment with these only if you truly enjoy scraping melted cheese from the ashes of a Weber. We're using dense, simple cheeses with a high melting point: think *cotija* or a ricotta salata on the hard and salty side for best results. *Queso blanco,* paneer, or halloumi will get misshapen, but they yield a softer bite and they will also survive the heat. If you're using a gas grill rather than charcoal, I suggest using some hickory sawdust to add to the smoke flavor (I get mine from SausageMaker.com).

1 (10-ounce) piece *cotija* cheese or ricotta salata

INSTRUCTIONS Open the top and bottom vents of a barbecue grill and light a moderate amount of mesquite hardwood coals; enough to fill a chimney starter halfway. In 20 to 30 minutes, the flames in the coals will have died down and they will be glowing and turning white. Pour the coals into one side of the grill: we want the cheese to smoke over indirect heat and not grill over high, direct heat.

If you're using a gas grill, heat one side of the grill to low heat. Scoop 3 cups of hickory sawdust into the middle of a large sheet of aluminum foil. Wrap the foil around the sawdust as if you were wrapping a present; the result should be a flat, square pack. Flip it over, and using the tip of a knife, stab about 15 small holes into the package to allow smoke from the sawdust to escape. Place the foil pack, holes side up, directly onto the grill's lava rocks or grill plate.

Lay a large piece of heavy-duty aluminum foil on the rack on the "cool" side of the grill, and place the cheese on top. Cover the grill, positioning the open vents over the cheese.

Allow the cheese to smoke undisturbed for 30 to 40 minutes, until the top appears golden in color and it is redolent of smoke. Using two wooden spoons or spatulas, flip the cheese, cover the grill again in the same manner, and let it smoke for another 20 to 30 minutes, until the other side is golden.

The cheese is ready to eat immediately: serve on a cheese plate, crumble over salad or winter squash, or coarsely grate into pasta.

HOW TO STORE IT Fully cooled and wrapped in plastic, it will keep for a month in the refrigerator.

10 | munch it

For some of us, there are merely two food groups: 1) food that comes in a crinkly bag meant to be ingested by the handful; and 2) everything else. We are a tribe of eternal snackers. Some of our best meals happen between meals.

Certainly every time you crave to dip a chip, you're not going to bust out the wok and start deep-frying the contents of your cupboard. However, when special occasions, rainy days, movie nights, birthday parties, and the need to gift strike, these haute snacks will fill the bill. Do the math: real food + real snacking = pure joy. No crinkly sack required.

soft pretzels

Makes 12 pretzels

TIME COMMITMENT
about 4 hours

While I love a crunchy rod or stick as much as the next gal, soft pretzels are the go-to carb-and-salt snack to make at home—because few things on this earth taste this good. And while they are at their best fresh, they are still delightful the next day—just rub them with a bit of water and re-bake for a few minutes. The most difficult part of this recipe will be waiting to devour them until they are really and truly cool; the flavor and crust just don't develop until they have rested for a full 30 minutes. Eat without mustard at your own risk. Oh, and feel free to track down fancy pretzel salt if you wish. Straight-up kosher salt works fine for me.

6 cups (1 pound, 13 ounces) all-purpose flour, plus more as needed

1 packet (2 1/2 teaspoons) active dry yeast

2 tablespoons sugar

1 tablespoon kosher salt, plus more for sprinkling

2 tablespoons vegetable oil

8 cups water

1/2 cup baking soda

1 egg

INSTRUCTIONS In a food processor fitted with the dough blade (or a stand mixer fitted with the dough hook), whirl together the flour, yeast, sugar, and salt. With the motor running (at low speed for a stand mixer), drizzle in the oil, then 2 cups of the water. The dough will come together and grab onto the dough hook.

Dust a countertop with flour and knead the dough, pushing it in from the sides and then over from the bottom, for 7 to 10 minutes. It will become less sticky, more cohesive, and slightly shiny, and it will have the texture of an earlobe to the touch. (If it doesn't, add more flour, 1 tablespoon at a time.)

Lightly oil a large bowl and dampen a clean kitchen towel. Heat a cup of water in the microwave and remove it. Roll the dough into a ball, transfer to the oiled bowl, and cover the bowl with the moist towel. Move the bowl into the microwave and let it sit for 1 hour.

Transfer the dough to a countertop lightly dusted with more flour. Stick your finger directly into the center to make a small hole. Use your fingers to widen the hole and work the dough, hand over hand as if you're pulling on a rope, into a large O-shape about 2 inches thick.

Cut the dough into a long rope and then into 12 equal pieces. Working with 1 dough piece at a time, roll into a 22-inch-long rope and fold into a pretzel shape: first, make a tall, skinny U shape, then cross the ends down and across each other to the opposite sides of the U. Pinch the pretzel to hold its shape. Form the other pretzels and let them rest for 20 minutes.

Preheat the oven to 425°F. Line 2 baking sheets with parchment paper.

// CONTINUED

soft pretzels, CONTINUED

Bring the remaining 6 cups of water and the baking soda to a rapid boil in a wide-mouthed Dutch oven or other large pot.

Boil the pretzels, one at a time, for 30 seconds each. Don't skip this step: it's what sets a pretzel apart from a doughy roll. Remove the pretzels from the water with a slotted spoon and hold them over the pot to drain well, then place them on the lined baking sheets. Beat the egg with 1 teaspoon of water. Brush the pretzels with this egg wash and sprinkle with salt to taste.

Bake both sheets of pretzels for 15 to 18 minutes, rotating the baking sheets and swapping their places in the oven halfway through. When they're done, the pretzels will be golden brown. Transfer to a cooling rack and allow them to cool for a full 30 minutes—really: this sets their texture.

HOW TO STORE IT The pretzels are ready to eat immediately, and they are best eaten within a day. Alternatively, they can be frozen in a zip-top bag for up to 3 months.

cheese weasels

Makes about 5 ounces
(about 2 cups)

TIME COMMITMENT
about 3 days

Silly name, severe crunchability. Centuries from now, historians will look back through the annals of culinary history. They will scour Brillat-Savarin and Escoffier, they will comb through the writings of M.F.K. Fisher and Michael Pollan, and they will look to one another with a single critical question burning in their hearts: Is it possible to make your own cheese doodles? The answer, my snacking friends, is "yes." Take this on on a rainy afternoon; you will not be disappointed. These do have a short shelf-life; I assure you this will not be an issue.

3 ounces Cheddar cheese

1 1/2 teaspoons kosher salt

3 teaspoons nutritional yeast

3 1/2 teaspoons nonfat milk powder

1/2 cup masa harina

1/4 teaspoon cayenne pepper (optional)

1 tablespoon butter, melted

1/2 cup plus 1 tablespoon water

2 cups neutral vegetable oil

INSTRUCTIONS First, the cheese must be dried out to become a powder. Using a sharp knife or a mandoline, slice the cheese very thinly, about 1/8 inch thick. Lay the cheese slices on a wire rack over a pan, not touching and not covered, so there's plenty of room for air to circulate around it. Let the cheese dry at room temperature until it becomes very hard and crumbly; depending on the humidity, this will take 2 to 3 days. Note that oil will rise to the surface of the cheese as it loses moisture; this is fine.

Once the cheese is completely hard, blot the oil with paper towels. Move the cheese to a food processor fitted with the metal blade and grind for 2 to 3 minutes, until it becomes a fine powder, scraping down the sides as needed. Measure out 1/2 cup of the cheese powder and return it to the processor bowl. Reserve the remaining cheese powder, if any, for another use.

Lightly pulse the cheese powder with 1 teaspoon of the salt, 2 teaspoons of the nutritional yeast, and 1 1/2 teaspoons of the milk powder. This will be the dusty coating of the cheese weasels: scrape it into a small brown paper bag and set aside.

In another bowl, use a fork to combine the masa harina, the remaining 2 teaspoons of the milk powder, the remaining 1 teaspoon of the nutritional yeast, and the remaining 1/2 teaspoon of the salt. (If you like, 1/4 teaspoon of cayenne added here will give your weasels some heat.) Stir in the melted butter, and then the water, and let this mixture rest for 5 minutes.

Set a rack over paper bags, newspaper, or paper towels on the countertop. Heat the oil in a 12-inch skillet over medium-high heat (the oil should be about 1/3 inch deep).

// CONTINUED

cheese weasels, CONTINUED

Using a scraper, transfer the dough into a quart-sized zip-top bag (or, if you have one, a pastry bag fitted with a narrow tip). When the oil is just starting to smoke, snip a very small corner from the bottom of the bag—just enough to allow a bit of the weasel batter to squeeze through. Working in batches, squeeze the dough directly into the hot oil in whatever shape you desire: I like 3-inch squiggly lines. Let the weasels fry for about 2 minutes, until golden; there's no need to flip them. Using tongs or a slotted spoon, gently remove them from the oil, allowing excess oil to drip back into the pan, and put them on the cooling rack until all the batter has been fried.

Move the still-warm fried weasels into the paper bag with the cheese dust. Shake gently to coat each weasel in cheesy dusting powder. Serve immediately or eat within the day.

HOW TO STORE IT Store in an open, paper-lined bowl for up to 3 hours.

fried pork rinds

Makes about 14 ounces

TIME COMMITMENT
about 14 hours

This is a high-ventilation, high-mess recipe, and one that feels almost daredevil for the home cook. But it's worth it! Homemade pork rinds are insanely tasty, and the way they puff up seems like a feat of kitchen magic. This is probably one of the healthiest parts of the pig to ingest—the animal fat is rendered away and the skin is cooked quickly in vegetable oil so hot that it barely soaks in—but whether it will become part of your daily diet is between you and your medical consultants. Making pork rinds requires two steps: first a lengthy rendering of the fat from the skin and then the actual frying, which goes very quickly. I encourage you to obtain the best pig skin you can from your local butcher that specializes in sustainable meats. Oh, and don't worry if there's still hair attached to the skin. This will burn off in the frying. ¡Viva los chicharrones!

1 pound pig skin
2 tablespoons kosher salt
5 cups neutral vegetable oil

INSTRUCTIONS Preheat the oven to 200°F.

Using a sharp knife and cutting along the underside of the skin, remove as much fat from the skin as you possibly can. Generously salt the skin on both sides and place it, fat side down, on a rack set over a rimmed baking sheet; put in the oven.

The point here is to render as much of the fat from the skin as possible and to dry the skin out until it's hard. After 7 to 8 hours, take the skin from the oven and use a spoon to scrape off the softened fat and discard. Return the skin to the oven for another 3 to 5 hours, after which all of the fat should be melted away and the skin should be hard and solid throughout. Once the skin is cool enough to handle, use your hands to crack it into 2-inch pieces. (At this point,

the skin can be stored airtight in the refrigerator or freezer for up to 4 months.)

In a wok with a candy or frying thermometer attached, heat the oil over medium-high heat until it starts to smoke and reaches 360°F, 5 to 8 minutes. Line your countertop or a baking sheet with paper bags, paper towels, or newspaper for draining, and have some tongs ready.

Working in batches of about 5 rinds at a time—they will puff up to be much larger than their current size—carefully place the rinds in the oil and swirl them around for 30 seconds until they puff dramatically. Remove them from the oil and let drain in a single layer on the paper. Taste the pork rinds before adding additional seasoning, as the salt level should be sufficient.

The rinds are ready to eat immediately.

HOW TO STORE IT Stored airtight at room temperature, they will last for up to 3 days.

crunchy lentil snacks

Makes about 3 cups

TIME COMMITMENT
up to 1 day

Gather 'round, ye skeptics. These lentils are not the mushy, bland vegetarian pabulum that has poisoned America. These are light, crunchy, immensely flavorful, and sort of fun and dangerous to make. If, like me, you're addicted to the panoply of bagged crunchy Indian snack mixes, these supercrunchers will soon send you to a snacker's twelve-step program as you combine them with nuts, raisins, and the Puffed Rice on page 17. Note that a slotted spoon cannot be used for this recipe. You will need a mesh skimmer capable of withstanding wickedly hot oil. And it's imperative that the lentils are COMPLETELY dry before frying. In oil this hot, any bit of water becomes a scalding, splattering mess.

2 cups brown lentils

2 cups neutral vegetable oil

2 teaspoons curry powder, either homemade (page 36) or store-bought

1/2 teaspoon kosher salt

INSTRUCTIONS Line a baking sheet with kitchen towels; set aside. In a large stockpot, bring about 10 cups of water to a boil over high heat. Slowly pour in the lentils, cover tightly, lower the heat as necessary to simmer for 15 minutes, until the lentils are tender but not thoroughly cooked.

Drain the lentils in a fine-mesh sieve, running them under cold water to cool thoroughly, and drain them well. Lay the lentils out in a single layer on the towel-lined baking sheet. Either let them dry overnight, stirring them occasionally; blow them dry with a hair dryer; or put them in the oven on its lowest possible setting for about an hour, stirring every 15 minutes, until they're completely dry.

Meanwhile, cover the countertop or another large baking sheet with clean newspaper or paper towels. Have at the ready a mesh skimmer suitable for removing foods from hot oil.

Place a wok over high heat, add the oil, and let it get smoking hot, about 5 minutes. When you see the smoke, quickly and CAREFULLY pour half of the dried lentils into the oil and stir. Turn off the heat, keep stirring, and allow the lentils to cook for 1 to 2 minutes total, just until some of the lentils turn mahogany brown. Remove the lentils from the oil as quickly as possible and spread them out on the paper to drain. Turn the heat back on, get the oil smoking hot again, and follow suit with the remaining lentils.

Once the lentils are cool, transfer them to a bowl, add the curry powder and salt, and toss to coat. Eat immediately.

HOW TO STORE IT Kept airtight at room temperature, these will last for at least 1 month.

caramel popcorn

Makes about 9 cups

TIME COMMITMENT
about 1 hour

This homemade spin on Cracker Jacks makes for a very well-received prezzie (you will need to supply your own tiny toy in a plastic wrapper). Not only is it an insanely great treat, but also because there is absolutely no way you should eat this entire recipe by yourself. (Trust me. You'll be sorry.) Don't skip the final baking time: I know it's more dishes to wash, but it makes a huge difference—the results are super-duper crunchy. Gift this tied up in lovely fabric lined with plastic wrap, tucked inside a paper towel tube wrapped in decorative paper, or in a good ol' fashioned pretty bag.

1$^1/_4$ cups popcorn
6 tablespoons neutral vegetable oil
1$^1/_2$ cups sugar
$^1/_2$ cup butter (1 stick)
1 tablespoon kosher salt

INSTRUCTIONS First, pop the corn. In a large stockpot with a lid, heat together the popcorn and the oil over medium heat. Wearing potholders, shake the pot occasionally over the heat until the corn starts to pop, at which point, you should shake the pot every 5 seconds to avoid scorching. Keep shaking until there's a 2-second pause between pops. At this point, turn off the heat and keep shaking constantly for another 30 to 60 seconds, until all popping subsides. Remove the lid carefully: the steam is very hot, and you may be attacked by a stray kernel! Pour the corn into a very large mixing bowl (or 2 smaller bowls if that's all you have): you will need a lot of room to mix the caramel into the corn. You should have 9 cups of popped corn. Resist eating it all.

Preheat the oven to 300°F and lightly oil 2 rimmed baking sheets.

In a small saucepan over medium heat, melt the sugar and let it caramelize without stirring for about 20 minutes, until it turns a beaver brown. Then, add the butter and stir it in until melted and smooth. Take the pan off the heat and stir in the salt.

Slowly and evenly pour the liquid caramel over the popcorn and toss with a wooden spoon at first, and then with your hands (moistened with water to prevent sticking) once it's cool enough, until well-coated.

Pour half of the caramel corn onto each baking sheet and spread it out evenly in a single layer. Bake the popcorn for 20 minutes, stirring the contents after 10 minutes, until the corn becomes crispy and darkens in hue slightly.

Let the popcorn cool completely before ingesting ludicrously.

HOW TO STORE IT If kept airtight, caramel corn will keep beautifully for at least 5 days at room temperature.

11 | sweeten it

Okay, Candy Girls and Boys: gimme some sugar. Or honey. Or caramel. Or sweetness in any form. Anyone can turn out cookies or a cake for immediate eating. What I've focused on here are sweet treats that can be made now and enjoyed right now *and* next week. Whatever you're into—chocolate, fruit, or spicy sweets—there is something here guaranteed to put your dentist to work. And hoard them as you wish—there will be plenty to share.

These candies and sweet spreads are designed to be eminently gift-ready. Lovely packages wrapped in ornate origami paper, pretty little jars, or whatever else you have tucked in your art cabinet should now come out to play.

chocolate hazelnut spread

Makes about 3 cups

TIME COMMITMENT
about 45 minutes

Spoon it, smear it, spread it on bread: there isn't a wrong way to eat *gianduja*, the Italian blended spread of toasted hazelnuts and rich chocolate. Essentially, you make your own chocolate sauce and your own hazelnut butter, and then combine the two. Unlike the popular commercial brand Nutella, a science-fictionally creamy whipped concoction drenched with modified palm oil and emulsifiers, this homemade version actually contains food you'd want to eat—though it isn't quite as shelf-stable. For the chocolate, I recommend something high quality like Valrhona, Callebaut, or Scharffen Berger over the standard chocolate chip. Note that a food processor is required for this recipe.

3 cups hazelnuts

3 ounces best-quality unsweetened dark chocolate, chopped (about 3/4 cup)

3 tablespoons butter, cubed

3/4 cup sugar

1 teaspoon vanilla extract, homemade (page 30) or store-bought

2 tablespoons vegetable oil

1 1/2 teaspoons kosher salt

INSTRUCTIONS Place a metal mixing bowl in the freezer to chill. Toast the nuts in a dry skillet over medium heat for about 8 minutes, until they're light golden brown. Pour them into the cold bowl and stir for 1 or 2 minutes. When they are cool enough to handle, rub the nuts to peel off as much of the outer husks as possible—don't worry if they don't all come off. Discard the husks. Allow the nuts to cool while you make the chocolate sauce.

In a small saucepan over medium-low heat, melt the chocolate with the butter and sugar, stirring frequently, about 3 minutes or until smooth and well combined (note that the sugar will still be somewhat coarse). Take the pan off the heat and continue stirring for about 30 seconds to cool slightly. Stir in the vanilla.

Transfer the nuts to a food processor fitted with the metal blade and whirl for 1 minute to make a thick paste. Scrape down the sides of the bowl; then, with the machine running, stream in the oil and continue to process for a full 5 minutes, until very smooth. With the machine still running, stream the chocolate sauce into the nut butter, using a rubber spatula to really scrape out the pan, and continue to whirl to combine well, about another 2 minutes. Add the salt to the spread and blend briefly to incorporate.

You can eat the spread immediately, but note that it's even better the next day.

HOW TO STORE IT It will keep at room temperature for up to 3 days. For longer storage (up to 3 months), refrigerate it, removing it from the fridge for 1 hour before eating and stirring it well right before use.

caramel

Makes about 12 ounces

TIME COMMITMENT
about 1 1/2 hours

If you botch a recipe of caramel, you should still love yourself, as there are worse things that could happen in the kitchen. If it cooks for too long, you have hard toffee; not long enough, and you have an excellent caramel syrup or spread. At the same time, making candy is all about temperature, and a candy or frying thermometer that clips to the side of your straight-sided pot is the only foolproof way to ensure that your caramel will be caramel. Note that this caramel is darker than your average store-bought squares. Feeling gifty? Feel free to finish off your individually wrapped caramels with fancy metallic twist ties, elegant foil, or tiny bands of pretty origami paper. And I personally pity the fool who does not smile at the gift of a caramel apple.

1/2 cup sugar

1 cup water

1 cup heavy whipping cream

1/4 cup honey

1/2 teaspoon kosher salt

1/4 teaspoon vanilla extract, homemade (page 30) or store-bought

INSTRUCTIONS First, make some simple syrup. In a medium saucepan with straight sides, combine the sugar and water and heat over medium heat just until all of the sugar dissolves, 2 to 3 minutes. Transfer the syrup to another vessel—like a glass jar. The syrup can be covered and kept refrigerated up to a week in advance.

Thoroughly oil an 8 by 8-inch baking dish.

Using the same (straight-sided) pan you used for the syrup, attach a candy thermometer to the side, being careful not to allow the sensor to touch the bottom of the pan. Pour the cream into the pan and heat over medium-high heat until it starts to bubble, about 3 minutes. Add the honey, 3/4 cup of the simple syrup (reserving the remaining syrup for another use), and the salt. Stir frequently with a wooden spoon until the temperature reaches 255°F, 15 to 18 minutes. Note that the mixture will foam and increase in volume; this is fine.

Once 255°F has been achieved, remove the pan from the heat and stir to cool slightly. Stir in the vanilla. Scrape the caramel into the prepared baking dish and allow it to cool, undisturbed, for 30 minutes. Then using a sharp knife or a pizza cutter dipped in water, score the caramel into bite-size pieces (or whatever shape you desire), separate the pieces, and store them, not touching, between sheets of wax paper or parchment paper. Or, to be extra fancy, wrap each caramel individually.

HOW TO STORE IT Keep the candy in an airtight container. In a dry climate, caramel will be at its best for a week at room temperature. In a humid climate, store caramel in the fridge for 2 weeks.

// CONTINUED

PLUS: caramel apples

Makes 4 caramel apples

INSTRUCTIONS Before you make the caramel, wash, dry, and stem 4 small, tart, crisp apples—Granny Smiths are perfect. Line a small baking sheet with parchment paper. Insert frozen pop sticks or trimmed, wooden barbecue skewers through the top of each apple and halfway through into the core, and place the apples on the lined baking sheet.

Make the caramel following the recipe on page 111 up until the point where you'd pour it into a pan. After you have added the vanilla and the caramel has cooled for 70 to 90 seconds, grab a stick and dunk the apple into the caramel, twirling it around and tipping the pan or spooning the caramel as necessary to cover the fruit. Lift the apple from the caramel and turn it upside down momentarily to let its surface smooth out, then replace it on the baking sheet, bottom side down and stick in the air.

Let the apples cool completely, at least 1 hour. To store, gently peel the apples from the parchment paper and wrap them in large squares of wax paper or parchment paper; close with a twist tie or pretty tape around the stick.

HOW TO STORE IT Well-wrapped, caramel apples will keep for up to 5 days at room temperature or refrigerated for up to 2 weeks.

dulce de leche

Makes about 4 cups

TIME COMMITMENT
about 8 hours

If you've never had the pleasure of this super caramel-y Argentinean treat, you may now take a number, line up, and join the ranks of those of us who cannot live without it. Use it where you would lemon curd: on top of your toast, spread between two cookies, swirled into ice cream, or schmeared onto pound cake or banana bread. You will also not be alone if you simply eat it with a spoon in front of the open refrigerator door. The ingredients are simple—it's your patience that will get a workout. While most recipes begin with canned sweetened condensed milk, I prefer to wait it out for the clean flavor of fresh (and organic) milk.

2 quarts whole milk

1 1/2 cups sugar

1 teaspoon vanilla extract, homemade (see page 30) or store-bought

INSTRUCTIONS Use a double boiler if you have one. If not, place a metal bowl over a large pot: the bowl should not be sitting in the bottom of the pot, and it should also cover the top of the pot completely, so no steam can escape. Fill the pot with as much water as possible without spilling over when the bowl is in position and bring the water to a boil over high heat. Reduce to a strong simmer, set the bowl in place on top of the pot, and pour the milk and sugar into the bowl. Stir to combine and dissolve the sugar as the mixture warms.

The milk needs to reduce for about 8 hours. As it cooks, scrape the sides and bottom of the bowl often with a sturdy wooden spoon or bowl scraper, increasing your frequency as the milk reduces. The color will turn from white to beige to caramel. Pay particular attention after about 6 hours of cooking time, when the milk will become viscous and require more frequent stirring attention.

At hour 7, put a couple of small plates into the freezer to cool. The dulce de leche is ready when it turns a deep caramel color, and when the milk is so thick that it coats the spoon in a thick layer. You can also test for doneness with the cold plate test: take a plate from the freezer and drop about 2 teaspoons of the dulce de leche onto the plate. Wait for 30 seconds and tip the plate vertically. If the mixture stays in place, it's ready. If it runs on the plate, keep reducing it further, and test again with the second plate.

Once the dulce de leche has reached the proper consistency, remove it from the heat. Stir for 1 minute to let it cool slightly, then stir in the vanilla. Pour into clean jars while it's still hot; this will minimize air bubbles.

HOW TO STORE IT Refrigerated, dulce de leche will last for at least 6 months.

candied citrus peel

Makes about 1 1/2 ounces

TIME COMMITMENT
about 1 hour

I heart Campari, I long for grapefruit—I love anything that's both bitter and sweet simultaneously. If you share my sense of tongue-tango culinary adventure, then this tasty snack is for you. Eat candied citrus peel straight up, dip it in chocolate, garnish a cocktail with it, chop it finely into the Caramel on page 111 or into the granolas on pages 19 or 21. Oh, and while I prefer this with orange peel, it also works with other citrus fruits (lemon, pomelo, grapefruit, and so on).

4 oranges, washed and dried
1/2 cup sugar
3/4 cup water

INSTRUCTIONS Using a vegetable peeler, remove the top layer of skin on the oranges, avoiding as much of the white pith below as possible. Reserve the oranges for another use (they are great for a quick glass of juice!). Cut the zest into 1 1/2-inch-long pieces.

Bring 2 small saucepans of water to a boil—boiling the rind will help remove some of its bitterness. In one pan, boil the zest for 1 minute. Drain and discard the liquid, and put the peels into the second pan. Boil the peels for an additional minute. Drain and discard the liquid.

Combine the peels with the sugar and water in a small saucepan (you can use one of the pans you used for boiling). Cover and bring the mixture to a boil over high heat. Reduce the heat to low, uncover, and simmer, stirring occasionally, about 25 minutes, pressing down on the skins as needed to make sure that they are covered in the syrup for the entire cooking time. Simmer until almost all of the liquid evaporates and the skins are covered in thick syrup speckled with bubbles.

Meanwhile, lightly oil a wire rack and place it over a baking sheet. Have tongs or chopsticks at the ready.

Test the peel for doneness by moving a single piece to the cooling rack, using the tongs or chopsticks. Crystals should form on the outside within 30 seconds of being removed from the pot. If not, keep cooking the peels and letting the sugar solution reduce further. Test again, and when the peels are done, work quickly to transfer the pieces, one by one, to the rack—don't let them touch one another on the rack. Careful: the candy will be very hot! Allow to cool for 10 to 15 minutes.

HOW TO STORE IT Enjoy immediately, or store in a paper towel–lined airtight container in the pantry for up to 3 months.

crystallized ginger

Makes about 7 ounces

TIME COMMITMENT
about 1 day

Sometimes it's fun to just blow up your palate. There are a lot of ways to do this, and the payoff is the pleasure that results from spicy hot or super sour bites. The pleasurable burn of fresh ginger mellowed by a sugar crust holds that sort of reward: think of it as a high dive for your taste buds. This is a full-flavored candy on its own, but it also gives a hearty oom-pah-pah to cookies, candies, quick breads, and so on. And while I would never pass myself off as someone qualified to offer medical advice, in my own personal experience, this is an entirely tasty panacea for nausea, morning sickness, and motion sickness. I prefer it sliced thin and on the crunchy side, but if you prefer it cubed and more chewy, chop accordingly.

8 ounces fresh ginger
3 1/2 cups sugar
2 cups water

INSTRUCTIONS Peel the ginger and, using a mandoline or sharp knife, slice it very thinly: about 1/8 inch.

Bring 2 cups of the sugar and the water to a boil in a medium saucepan. Add the ginger, stirring to coat, lower the heat and simmer, uncovered, for 30 minutes. Turn off the heat, cover, and let steep for at least 2 hours or overnight.

Strain the liquids from the solids, retaining the strained ginger syrup for another use, such as stirring with sparkling water for a quick soda—refrigerated, it will keep for up to a week.

Pour the remaining 1 1/2 cups of sugar in with the drained ginger pieces and mix with your hands, coating every surface of the ginger with sugar: make certain the ginger pieces don't stick together.

Spread the ginger out in a single layer on a baking sheet and let it dry overnight, stirring once or twice.

HOW TO STORE IT Once it's completely dry, move it to an airtight container lined with a paper towel. The ginger will keep for up to a year in the refrigerator.

12 | milk it

To you I say, "Moo." Who am I to moo at you? A woman who finds alternative milks udderly intoxicating.

Don't get me wrong: I am a meat-avore and a dairy enthusiast. But as much as I would love to have old Bessie tied up in the backyard, I'm fairly certain that my neighbors would complain and my dachshund would go ballistic. If city life does not allow me to milk my own, the next best thing is for me to make my own milk.

Milks from nuts and beans are rich, flavorful, and versatile, useful in everything from a sauce to a sweet milkshake to fresh tofu (if you've never had the pleasure of eating fresh tofu curds, I encourage you two to meet). Some are a cinchy snap, while others are a bit more labor-intensive. But all are entirely worth the effort. Bessie, it's time for us to milk it.

almond milk

Makes about 3 1/2 cups

TIME COMMITMENT
at least 6 hours

I crave this on hot days just because it's insanely delicious and it makes me feel purely hydrated when I imbibe it. Kinda nutty, kinda creamy, it's a nice change on cereal, warmed up in your chai, or as a substitute for the milk in ice cream. My favorite, however, is drinking it straight from the Mason jar. Oh, and feel free to sweeten it up to your taste: a lot of people like to blend in dates, maple syrup, agave syrup, barley malt, or some other natural sugar. For me, almond milk is sweet enough on its own. While soaking the almonds yields a much sweeter, smoother, more full-flavored milk, you can get by in a pinch just using raw, dry almonds (or hazelnuts, or cashews). Note that a blender is required.

1 cup raw almonds
4 cups water

INSTRUCTIONS Soak the almonds in water to cover by 1 inch for at least 6 hours or overnight. They will plump up by about 30 percent while soaking.

Drain the almonds and place them and the water in the blender. Blend on the highest setting for a full 2 minutes.

Pour the milk through a fine-mesh strainer, pressing down on the solids as you go. Discard the solids and strain the milk one more time, this time not squeezing the solids.

The milk is ready to drink immediately: try it straight up or over ice.

HOW TO STORE IT Kept refrigerated, almond milk will last for 5 days. Frozen, it will last for up to 4 months.

rice milk

Makes about 4 cups

TIME COMMITMENT
at least 6 hours

If you've been buying that stuff in the carton, you've been paying like a sucker. A cup of rice and some tap water are all that's needed to produce a superfresh, superflavored dairy-free alternative for your morning bowl of flakes and more. Note that a blender is necessary for this recipe.

1 cup long-grain white rice

4 cups water

4 tablespoons sugar (optional)

INSTRUCTIONS Soak the rice in the water for at least 6 hours or overnight. Transfer the rice and the soaking liquid to the blender and whirl on its highest speed for a full 2 minutes. If you're using sweetener, blend it in with the rice. Strain through a fine-mesh strainer and discard the solids. Enjoy immediately, or serve cold or over ice.

HOW TO STORE IT Kept refrigerated, rice milk will last for up to 1 week. Frozen rice milk will keep for up to 4 months.

PLUS: *horchata*

INSTRUCTIONS As anyone who lives within sniffing distance of a taqueria can tell you, *horchata* is an outrageously enjoyable beverage made from rice milk. On a hot day and/or with hot food, its sweet cinnamon coolness is most welcome. To make it, make the Rice Milk and soak 1 (3-inch) cinnamon stick in the water along with the rice. Include the cinnamon stick in the blender when pureeing the rice, along with a pinch of kosher salt and 4 tablespoons of your favorite sugar or natural sweetener, adding more to taste. Strain and enjoy immediately, or serve cold or over ice.

HOW TO STORE IT *Horchata* will keep in the refrigerator for 3 days, but it does not freeze well.

coconut milk (two ways)

TIME COMMITMENT
1 1/2 to 2 hours

We have grown so used to coconut milk in cans that most of us don't even know what fresh coconut milk tastes like. Let me be the first to demystify this: homemade coconut milk actually tastes like coconut. For the record, I will also state that coconut milk should not be confused with coconut water, that addictive, refreshing clear beverage that comes from inside a young coconut. Nor should this be mistaken for cream of coconut, which is super-thick and sweet and is often used in desserts and creamy cocktails. This is coconut *milk*, the foundation of many an excellent curry. I present two options for making your own, depending on your level of geekdom. One starts with shredded store-bought coconut, and the other starts with the whole fresh nut. To go the latter route, be sure to purchase mature coconuts, often sold as brown orbs with the husks removed, sometimes labeled "coco seco." "Thai" coconuts or "young" coconuts aren't what you want for this job.

coconut milk from shredded coconut

Makes about 1 2/3 cups

2 cups water
2 cups shredded unsweetened coconut

INSTRUCTIONS In a small, covered saucepan, bring the water to a boil. Stir in the coconut, turn off the heat, cover, and let sit for 1 hour.

Once the coconut has steeped, pour the contents of the pan into a dishtowel-lined bowl. Gather all four corners of the towel and lift up the coconut mass, allowing the liquid to drip into the bowl beneath. Twist and squeeze the towel to harvest as much liquid as you can. Discard the solids. This liquid is your milk, and it's ready to be used in cooking.

HOW TO STORE IT Kept in an airtight container, coconut milk can be refrigerated for up to 5 days (however, note that it may separate after a couple of days and will need to be stirred before use). Frozen, it will last for up to 1 year.

coconut milk from whole coconuts

Makes about 2¹/₄ cups

  1 whole mature coconut
  3 cups water

INSTRUCTIONS Preheat the oven to 350°F.

First, drain the coconut's water. Take your coconut and find the eyes: the small brown circles near the top. With a hammer and a screw or nail, bang holes into two of the eyes (you need 2 holes to let the air in so the water can flow out). Pour the water directly into a drinking glass and refresh yourself; wielding a hammer is hard work.

Place the drained coconut into a large plastic bag (this will reduce the mess) and take it and the hammer outside. Shatter the giant nut into large pieces. Wrap the smashed coconut pieces tightly in aluminum foil and bake for 30 minutes. This will make very simple work of removing the nut from its shell.

Take the coconut pieces from the oven and, using a paring knife, remove the meat from the shell. Grate or finely chop the coconut by hand or in a food processor; you should have about 3 cups. In a saucepan, boil the 3 cups of water (or use an amount equal to your volume of coconut) and add the coconut. Lower the heat and simmer for 10 minutes, covered. Turn off the heat and let the coconut sit for 1 hour.

Line a bowl with a clean kitchen towel and pour the coconut mash and its liquid into the center. Bring the four corners of the towel together and lift the towel from the bowl; the coconut milk will drip out from the bottom. Tightly twist and squeeze the towel to release as much of the liquid as possible. The milk is now ready to use. Bonus: Your hands will be incredibly soft from the coconut fat.

HOW TO STORE IT Kept in an airtight container, coconut milk can be refrigerated for up to 5 days (however, note that it may separate after a couple of days and will need to be stirred before use). Frozen, it will last for up to 1 year.

soy milk

Makes about 9 cups

TIME COMMITMENT
about 15 hours

Whether you're enjoying this on cereal or in your coffee, or you're crafting the start to your own tofu (see opposite page), making your own soy milk is laborious but simple. Why there exists a cabinet-hogging device designed just for this purpose, I've not a clue: simply soak, blend, strain, and steam, and soy milk is yours. To make it taste more like the stuff you buy in a carton, add some sugar or other flavorings. Note that a blender or food processor is required for this recipe. Some people like to reserve the *okara*, the solid mass strained from the milk, and use it as a protein source for soups, breads, smoothies, and so on.

2 1/2 cups dried soybeans

INSTRUCTIONS Soak the soybeans in 8 cups of water for at least 12 hours but no more than 24. Drain the water and rinse the beans thoroughly.

Set a large fine-mesh sieve (or a colander lined with a thin kitchen towel) over a large bowl. In a blender or food processor, puree the beans in batches of 1 cup of beans with 1 1/2 cups of water, for 2 to 3 minutes per batch, ensuring that the beans are as pulverized as possible. (Sit back, relax, and enjoy the cracking sound.) Pour the mixture through the sieve into the bowl. Stir and press down on the solids to release as much liquid as possible, then discard them or set them aside for another purpose. Continue pureeing and straining in batches until the beans are all processed. You will likely need to remove the solids from the sieve several times during the straining process.

Wash out the sieve (or use a clean towel) and strain the soy milk a second time, moving it from the bowl to a heavy stockpot. Heat over medium-high heat until the soy milk starts to steam; don't let it boil. Stir often, as the soy milk can stick to the bottom and sides of the pan. Lower the heat

as needed to keep the milk steaming for 25 minutes, continuing to stir occasionally. It will now have a cooked flavor. At this point, your soy milk is ready to drink. If you're adding sweetener or other flavorings (see sidebar), add them during the last 5 minutes of cooking time and stir to combine.

Drink either warm or cold.

HOW TO STORE IT Refrigerated, the soy milk will keep for up to a week.

PLUS: sweetened, flavored soy milks

INSTRUCTIONS To make sweetened soy milk, add 1 1/2 teaspoons sugar for every cup of soy milk (or, if your plan is to sweeten the whole batch, add 1/4 cup sugar, and then an additional tablespoon to taste). Or, try 4 teaspoons honey, maple syrup, or chocolate syrup, and/or 1/4 teaspoon almond or vanilla extract, per cup of soy milk.

tofu

Time is no friend to tofu, and its flavor is absolutely the best when it's super-duper fresh. Similar to the way that milk becomes cheese, soybeans become tofu by first crafting soy milk, adding a coagulant to make curds, and then pressing the curds into shape. And while this isn't a practical dinner solution every night, the effort is entirely worth what you end up with; silken, soft, fresh tofu best prepared with the lightest hand (green onion, soy sauce, and a squeeze of lemon). Other coagulants exist for making tofu, but I far prefer the clean flavor of natural food-grade *nigari* (chemical name, magnesium chloride). It's pretty easy and inexpensive to find online; I buy mine from GEMCultures.com. Feel free to shell out for a fancy cheese press or a classic square wooden tofu press. I prefer to use an empty 28-ounce can with both lids removed.

9 cups unflavored, unsweetened soy milk, homemade (opposite page) or store-bought

2 teaspoons *nigari* (magnesium chloride)

INSTRUCTIONS In a large, uncovered Dutch oven, warm the soy milk over medium heat until it starts to release steam; do not let it boil. Stir occasionally to keep the heat even. Allow the soy milk to steam for 10 minutes.

Remove 1/3 cup of the warmed soy milk from the pot and pour into a bowl. Add the *nigari* to the bowl, mixing well to dissolve and combine.

Slowly and evenly pour the *nigari* slurry back into the pot, mixing it in with a ladle or large spoon using an up-and-down motion to distribute the coagulant evenly throughout the soy milk. Turn off the heat, cover, and let sit for 5 minutes to allow the curds to form. If the milk is not curdled throughout, slowly and carefully stir up and down again in spots as necessary, being careful not to break up any existing curds. Cover again and let it sit for an additional 3 minutes.

Pour the contents of the pot through a fine-mesh sieve, discarding the strained-out liquid. Stir the curds lightly and let them drain for 20 minutes. The tofu curds are ready to eat immediately, and they are really delicious while still warm.

If you want to press the tofu into a round cake, fold a clean kitchen towel over a plate (this will help absorb the pressed liquid). Place an empty 28-ounce can with both lids cut out (and retained) on top (or use a tofu press or cheese press). Set the bottom lid in place and spoon the well-drained curds into the mold. Lay the second lid from the can (or the top of the press) over the curds and add some weight on top, such as a pint jar filled with water. The longer you let the tofu sit, the firmer it will become. For medium-firm tofu, let it sit for 2 hours.

Carefully remove the finished tofu from the press; it's ready to eat.

HOW TO STORE IT Tofu will keep, submerged in water and refrigerated, for up to 5 days.

13 | slurp it

The ultimate thumb-to-the-nose for the packaged foodstuffs industry is to eschew the bottles and cans whose brand names have come to be synonymous with soft drinks. Sure, their flavors are reliable, but they are heavy and sometimes caustic to produce, and they support a beverage monoculture that is just plain boring. Strip back the flashy labels and the marketing and what do you have? Sweet, flavored bubbles, which are certainly easy enough to brew up at home.

Home beverage curators tend to draw the line at lemonade and iced tea. While I would never speak poorly of these fine libations, there are other fruits and spices in the sea that merit your taste buds' attention.

strawberry black pepper syrup

Makes 3 1/4 to 4 cups

TIME COMMITMENT
less than 1 week

In truth, this is actually two recipes: a fruit syrup that is a stunning Day-Glo red starter for bubbling cold beverages (see photo on page 129), and also its by-product—my favorite strawberry jam to date. Absolutely do not discard the macerated fruit left over from making the syrup; when tossed in a food processor or food mill with a squeeze of orange juice, it's a jam that can be stored fresh in the refrigerator for a few days or canned for later. (The same is true for the other two syrups in this chapter: they give you syrup AND yummy jam.) Note that if you can this syrup, the flavor will become cooked but still makes a good soda.

About 2 pounds ripe organic strawberries, washed, hulled, and halved (7 cups)

3 1/2 cups sugar

3 tablespoons orange juice (about 1/2 orange)

2 tablespoons crushed black peppercorns

INSTRUCTIONS In a giant mixing bowl, combine the berries with 2 cups of the sugar, being sure to coat each berry in sugar completely. Cover the top of the berries in a blanket of the remaining 1 1/2 cups sugar. Let the berries macerate for 12 hours, stirring occasionally to help the sugar dissolve. (Setting this up after dinner and stirring periodically before bedtime is sufficient.) The berries will shrink in size and release their juice and the sugar will dissolve in the liquid. If necessary, cover the bowl loosely with a kitchen towel tied with string to protect the sweet syrup from insects.

After maceration, stir again to dissolve as much sugar as possible from the bottom of the bowl. Set a fine-mesh sieve over a bowl and drain the syrup into it, stirring the fruit (but not pressing on it) to release as much liquid as possible. Reserve the fruit for another use (like jam or pie filling) and taste your syrup. Heaven.

Stir in the orange juice and the peppercorns and transfer the mixture to a clean, odorless glass jar with a secure lid. Refrigerate for 5 to 6 days to allow the peppercorn flavor to develop.

HOW TO STORE IT Store, refrigerated, for up to 1 month. For long-term storage, pour into canning jars and process for 10 minutes (see directions for canning on page 28). Canned, it will keep for 1 year.

PLUS: strawberry black pepper soda (two ways)

INSTRUCTIONS Stir 3/4 cup Strawberry Black Pepper Syrup into 1 1/2 cups sparkling water (or any quantity in a ratio of 1:2). Add ice cubes and enjoy. Shot of gin optional. To make carbonated soda, see How to Carbonate It, opposite page. Drink within 3 days. Note that soda left for longer than that, even at cold temperatures, is in danger of becoming explosively overcarbonated.

HOW TO CARBONATE IT

In a clean glass bottle of any size with a tight-fitting lid, combine syrup and tap water in a ratio of 1:2—for example, a 750 ml bottle can hold a little more than 24 ounces, which means 8 ounces of syrup and 16 ounces of water. Add to the mix a scant pinch of active dry yeast, cap tightly, and shake well to combine. Label and date the bottle. Allow it to get gassy at room temperature for 1 to 3 days until carbonated. The best way to test for carbonation is to create one small "testing" bottle of soda that should be checked daily for proper carbonation. To do so, decant 1 to 2 ounces of your soda into a separate bottle, rescrewing the cap tightly after each check. Once the soda has achieved the right level of bubbles, move the bottle to the refrigerator and let the soda chill.

pineapple mint syrup

Makes about 2 1/2 cups

TIME COMMITMENT
about 1 day

I hate to play favorites because it just makes the other soda recipes jealous. But between, you, me, and the ice cubes, I must admit that this syrup makes one of my favorite home-made sodas. I return to it again and again. The mint comes on first, and then the sweet tropical fruit follows like a breeze. And before you throw away the rind from the pine-apple, check out the recipe for Tepache on page 132.

7 cups fresh pineapple chunks (from about a 2-pound fruit)

1 cup dark brown sugar

2 cups white sugar

1 bunch fresh mint, well washed

2 tablespoons fresh lemon juice (from 1 lemon)

INSTRUCTIONS Combine the pineapple and both sugars to coat in a large, covered pot and let it macerate, stirring occasionally to help the sugar dissolve, for at least 12 but no more than 24 hours. (Setting this up after dinner and stirring periodically before bedtime is sufficient.) The fruit will shrink in size and release its juice and the sugar will dissolve in the liquid. If necessary, cover the bowl loosely with a kitchen towel tied with string to protect the sweet syrup from insects.

When the fruit has macerated, move the pot to the stovetop. Tie the mint together at the stems with kitchen string or unwaxed, unflavored dental floss and dunk the leaves into the fruit and syrup. (Leaving the stems sticking out will help with easy removal later.) Cover the pot and bring to a gentle boil over high heat, then lower the heat and simmer for 3 minutes. Turn off the heat and let the mixture steep, still covered, for 30 minutes.

Remove the mint with tongs or your fingers and squeeze out as much of its liquid as you can through a sieve back into the pot. Strain the pineapple from the liquid and save it for another use (such as eating). Stir in the lemon juice.

HOW TO STORE IT Pour the syrup into a glass bottle for storing in the refrigerator, where it will keep for up to 6 weeks. For long-term storage, pour into canning jars and process for 10 minutes (see directions for canning on page 28). Canned, it will last for 1 year.

PLUS: pineapple mint soda (two ways)

INSTRUCTIONS Stir 3/4 cup Pineapple Mint Syrup into 1 1/2 cups sparkling water (or any quantity in a ratio of 1:2). Add ice cubes and enjoy. Shot of rum optional. To make carbonated soda, see How to Carbonate It, page 127. Drink within 5 days. Note that soda left longer for than that, even at cold temperatures, is in danger of becoming explosively overcarbonated.

Opposite page (left to right): Pineapple Mint Soda, Strawberry Black Pepper Soda, Blueberry Lemon Soda.

blueberry lemon syrup

Makes about 4 1/2 cups

TIME COMMITMENT
about 20 minutes

Tangy, tart, and blueberry-luscious, this syrup makes a drink with the most stunning purple color when illuminated by square ice cubes and the sun (see photo on page 129). This is your picnic soda, provided that you can keep it super chilled. Be certain you're using ripe, delicious berries good enough to eat out of hand. Of all the syrups in this chapter, this one best takes to canning for nonseasonal enjoyment.

4 1/2 cups fresh blueberries
2 cups sugar
2 cups water
3 tablespoons fresh lemon juice (from 1 or 2 lemons)
Pinch of kosher salt

INSTRUCTIONS Combine the fruit, sugar, and water in a large saucepan over medium heat and bring to a gentle boil (but be careful not to let it boil over). Reduce the heat and simmer, covered, for 3 minutes—just enough time to let the berries release their juice.

Take the pan off the heat and stir to cool slightly. Pour the contents of the pan through a fine-mesh sieve set over a large bowl, stirring but not pressing the berries to harvest as much syrup as possible.

Reserve the berries for another use. (But don't toss them out! Puree them in a blender to make a great jam, or use them as an ice cream topping, pie filling, or compote.) Stir the lemon juice and the salt into the syrup.

HOW TO STORE IT Using a funnel, pour the syrup into a glass bottle for storing in the refrigerator, where it will keep for up to 6 weeks. For long-term storage, pour into canning jars and process for 10 minutes (see directions for canning on page 28). Canned, it will last 1 year.

PLUS: blueberry lemon soda (two ways)

INSTRUCTIONS Stir 3/4 cup Blueberry Lemon Syrup into 1 1/2 cups sparkling water (or any quantity in a ratio of 1:2). Add ice cubes and enjoy. Shot of vodka optional. To make carbonated soda, see How to Carbonate It, page 127. Drink within 3 days. Note that soda left for longer for than that, even at cold temperatures, is in danger of becoming explosively overcarbonated.

british-style ginger beer

Makes about 6 cups

TIME COMMITMENT
up to 10 days

In my first book, *Jam It, Pickle It, Cure It*, I shared a recipe for a rockingly pungent Jamaican-style ginger beer frothed in a blender with loads of sugar and citrus. This is its fermented upper-crusty cousin. It's somewhat smoother and more refined, and delicately effervescent from the natural fermentation agent found on the ginger's skin. Note that this soda requires a double fermentation: first making the ginger beer starter (aka the "bug"), and then fermenting in the bottle. The result is pure liquid summer. You'll be grating some fresh ginger every day for about a week—a Microplane is the perfect tool, if you have one. Otherwise, use the small holes on a box grater.

6 cups water
About 9 teaspoons freshly grated ginger (with the skin)
About 9 teaspoons plus 1 cup sugar

INSTRUCTIONS First, create the ginger beer starter. In a clean 1 quart (or larger) jar or bowl, combine 2 cups of water with 3 teaspoons of freshly grated ginger and 3 teaspoons of sugar. Stir to combine. Cover the jar or bowl with a paper towel secured by a rubber band around the rim. You want to let air in but keep insects out.

The next day, add another teaspoon of freshly grated ginger and another teaspoon of sugar, stirring to combine and loosely covering again. Do this daily until the starter foams and releases a strong, fermenting odor; this can take up to 1 week.

Once you have your starter, strain it through a fine-mesh sieve into a large clear measuring cup, pressing hard on the solids as you go, and then discarding them. You should have somewhere in the neighborhood of 1 3/4 cups of liquid starter. Pour equal amounts of the starter through a funnel into 2 clean 750 ml (or larger)

bottles with tight-fitting caps. Into each bottle, also funnel in 1/2 cup of sugar and 2 cups of water. Cap the bottles tightly and shake them well to dissolve the sugar. Once the sugar has been absorbed, swirl the bottle around upright to ensure that there's no sugar coating the lip or neck of the bottle. Into a smaller third bottle, which will serve as your "tester" bottle, pour 1/2 ounce from each bottle.

Label and date the bottles and let them sit at room temperature for 1 to 3 days—warmer weather will yield faster carbonation. Check the tester bottle after every 24-hour period for your preferred level of fermentation. Be sure to recap the tester tightly between tests, and know that the ginger beer in the unopened bottles will lean slightly fizzier than that in your tester.

HOW TO STORE IT Once the ginger beer in the tester is properly carbonated, move the bottles to the refrigerator, chill, and drink within 5 days. Note that soda left for longer than that, even at cold temperatures, is in danger of becoming explosively overcarbonated.

tepache

Makes about 5 cups

TIME COMMITMENT
about 5 days

Okay, I admit this to you, cookbook author to cookbook purchaser: I wavered on whether or not to include this recipe. As I understand it, this is an old-fashioned summer cooler, a natural and economical use of pineapple rind before it hits the compost bin, and a popular basis for hooch in Mexican prisons (it's just barely alcoholic in this recipe; you'd have to let it go for much longer to get soused). I'm a big fan of its dry fruit and natural swampiness, but many of those who have crossed my kitchen threshold don't share my enthusiasm. I say give it a whirl, as it's a fun project to do with something you would normally have cast aside. Additionally, if you ever find yourself behind bars in Tijuana, you'll be able to dazzle your cellmates with your culinary chops.

2 1/2 cups dark brown sugar
Rind and core of 1 whole pineapple (minus the green leaves), coarsely chopped
2 (3-inch) cinnamon sticks

INSTRUCTIONS In a large glass, ceramic, or food-grade plastic container, pour the sugar over the pineapple rind and stir well to coat each piece of rind in sugar. Nestle the cinnamon into the pineapple rind until it's buried. Pour 2 to 3 cups of tap water over all of it, until the water just covers the fruit.

Cover the top of the container loosely with a kitchen towel and tie a string around it to secure it: you want to keep insects out but allow airflow in. Allow it to ferment for 2 to 4 days, checking it daily: you want to see just natural bubbles, not a thick layer of mold.

Once bubbles have formed, strain it through a fine-mesh sieve set over a bowl. Discard the solids. Pour the liquid into 2 clean 750 ml bottles, diluting the tepache 1:1 (for every cup of tepache, dilute with 1 cup of water). Into a smaller third bottle, which will serve as your "tester" bottle, pour 1/2 ounce from each bottle. Cap the bottles tightly and allow them to sit at room temperature for 1 to 3 days, until the liquid in the tester bottle becomes carbonated.

Once the liquid is bubbling to your liking, transfer the bottles to the refrigerator and chill until very cold, then serve immediately over ice.

HOW TO STORE IT Refrigerate and consume within 2 to 3 days—this is not a beverage for aging longer than that.

apple cider

Makes 4 quarts

TIME COMMITMENT
about 2 hours

A blend of apples (three or more sweet varieties) gives this drink a nice complexity and roundness. Score an apple bargain at the farmers' market of ugly or mealy fruit, but avoid the rotten specimens fallen from the tree, as their bruised or rotten flavor will seep into the juice. This is delicious both ice cold and gently warmed. Cinnamon or not is up to you.

5 pounds each (15 pounds total) of three sweet apple varieties, such as Fuji, Honeycrisp, Candy Crisp, Arkansas Black, or Red Delicious

INSTRUCTIONS This recipe requires some hardware assembly. Find a large bowl or food-safe bucket and place a sturdy rack on top. Line a large colander or sieve with a thin, clean kitchen towel, and place this colander on top of the rack. The point is to leave room to collect as much juice as possible in the bowl. Note that if you don't have a cooling rack large enough to sit atop the bowl, you can use a clean oven rack.

Wash, quarter, and core the apples, leaving the skins intact. Puree the apples in batches in a food processor or blender, along with about 1/3 cup of water per batch—just enough to get the blades going. Process for 1 minute, scrape down the sides if necessary, then process for 1 minute longer. The apples should be completely pulverized.

Pour each batch of pureed apples into the towel-lined colander. Allow the juice to drip through to the bowl beneath, stirring and pressing on the mash periodically to help harvest as much juice as possible. Note that you will need to empty the towel of its contents at least one time during the processing, as all of the pureed fruit won't fit. To do this, bring together the four corners of the towel and twist it into a hard ball to squeeze out all the juice. Loosen the towel, stir the mash, and squeeze again a couple more times to harvest as much juice as possible. Discard the solid fruit.

Continue until all the apples have been juiced, squeezing the puree in the towel again at the end. Note that the juice will darken as you work.

Refrigerate the collected liquid immediately and drink within 5 days. To keep cider longer, heat to 160°F for pasteurization and keep refrigerated for up to 2 weeks. (Note that heating the juice will alter its flavor.)

HOW TO STORE IT For longer-term storage, can the juice by pouring into pint or quart jars and processing for 15 minutes (see directions for canning on page 28). Or freeze the juice, being careful to leave 1/2 inch of headspace in each container to allow for expansion of the liquid. Both of these methods will preserve the juice for up to 1 year.

14 freeze it

Chilly. The pantry is packed, the fridge is full, but the freezer? Is there anything in there beyond a forgotten frozen casserole, a bottle of vodka, and an echo?

The freezer is a veritable no-man's-land of kitchen project creativity. Few venture forth into its ultracold confines—yet it is capable of churning out scoopable ice cream and a plethora of frozen novelties that will reward and impress. And, surprisingly, you can make the magic happen with very little specialized equipment.

Why not take better advantage of this dark horse of the kitchen? Together, let us chill. . . .

orange vanilla cream pops

Makes six 4-ounce pops

TIME COMMITMENT
about 7 hours

These are so creamy, they're nearly ice cream. Still, that hit of citrus helps keep the cream in balance, and these are flavor on a stick. Many recipes opt for starting out with orange juice concentrate, but simply making your own juice reduction is an investment in pure flavor. The simplicity of the ingredients creates something far beyond the sum of its parts.

4 cups orange juice

6 tablespoons sugar

2 teaspoons vanilla extract, homemade (page 30) or store-bought

3/4 cup plus 1 tablespoon heavy cream

INSTRUCTIONS In a small uncovered saucepan over medium-high heat, boldly simmer the orange juice (but don't let it splatter), stirring occasionally, and reduce it to 2 cups, about 15 minutes. Once it's reduced, remove from the heat and stir to cool the juice slightly for about 3 minutes, then stir in the sugar, vanilla, and cream. Pour into six 4-ounce frozen pop molds and freeze for 6 hours. Be sure to leave 1/4 to 1/2 inch of headspace at the top of each pop mold to allow for the liquid's expansion in the freezer.

To release an individual pop, rotate it under a stream of running warm tap water for about 30 seconds. Never tug on the stick! Keep running it under water until the pop can be pulled out gently. (Should this fail, eat your pop from the mold with a spoon.)

HOW TO STORE IT Kept frozen and completely covered, these will last for up to 4 months.

salted margarita cream pops

Makes six 4-ounce pops

TIME COMMITMENT
about 7 hours

Sure, okay, twist my arm. You can use regular ol' limes if you want to. But here's why I think finding Key limes is worth the extra effort: these tiny yellow-greenish orbs commonly found at Latin American and Asian groceries have a creamy, super-extra-tangy flavor that makes the common lime hide under its rind in shame. Thanks to the booze, these are not kid-safe, though, to your own culinary peril, the tequila can be omitted if you wish. Please enjoy this full cocktail on a stick.

1/2 cup Key lime juice

2 teaspoons minced Key lime zest

3/4 cup water

7 ounces sweetened condensed milk (half of a 14-ounce can)

1 1/2 tablespoons tequila

2 teaspoons kosher salt

INSTRUCTIONS In a bowl, combine the lime juice, zest, water, condensed milk, and tequila and stir well. Divide the salt evenly into the bottom (later, it will be the top) of each of six 4-ounce frozen pop molds. Pour the margarita mixture into each mold, leaving about 1/2 inch headspace for the liquid's expansion in the freezer. Freeze for 6 hours, until solid.

To release an individual pop, rotate it under a stream of running warm tap water for about 30 seconds. Never tug on the stick! Keep running it under water until the pop can be pulled out gently. (Should this fail, eat your pop from the mold with a spoon.)

HOW TO STORE IT Kept frozen and completely covered, these will last for up to 4 months.

berry cabernet pops

Makes six 4-ounce pops

TIME COMMITMENT
about 6 hours

Wine, fruit, and a light dose of sweetness: these frozen pops are more Saturday night than Sunday morning. Why should children get all the brightly colored fun? For your next date night or cocktail party, unsheathe some of these. For the wine, don't go hog wild, but don't use the supercheap stuff, either. Cabernet Sauvignon or anything else that leans fruity will suffice.

3^1/2 cups frozen raspberries, strawberries, or blueberries, or a combination

^{3}/4 cup sugar

^{3}/4 cup medium-bodied fruity red wine

2 tablespoons fresh lemon juice (from 1 lemon)

INSTRUCTIONS Combine all the ingredients in a blender or food processor and blend for about 2 minutes, until completely liquefied. Pour into six 4-ounce frozen pop molds, leaving about ^{1}/2 inch headspace for the liquid's expansion. Freeze until solid, at least 6 hours.

To release an individual pop, rotate it under a stream of running warm tap water for about 30 seconds. Never tug on the stick! Keep running it under water until the pop can be pulled out gently. (Should this fail, eat your pop from the mold with a spoon.)

HOW TO STORE IT Kept frozen and completely covered, these will last for up to 4 months.

strawberry ice cream (without an ice cream maker)

Makes about 1 quart

TIME COMMITMENT
about 7 1/2 hours

Rid yourself of that enormous ice cream maker bogarting all the freezer space, I say, and rely instead on the tools you already have at hand. I encourage you to play with flavors and fold-ins for your own crazy ice cream concoctions. You'll find recipes for basic chocolate and vanilla below.

1 cup water

1 cup sugar

1/2 cup heavy whipping cream

1/2 cup whole milk

Pinch of kosher salt

1/2 cup strawberry jam

Pinch of minced orange zest

INSTRUCTIONS In a small saucepan over medium heat, combine the water and sugar and stir often for about 5 minutes, just until the sugar dissolves. Allow this syrup to cool completely before using. (Note that the syrup can be made up to a week ahead of time and kept, covered, in the refrigerator.)

In a large bowl with a tight-fitting lid, stir together the syrup, cream, milk, salt, jam, and zest. Cover and freeze for 2 hours. Remove from the freezer and aerate with a hand mixer on low speed for about 15 seconds. Cover and return to the freezer. Every hour for the next 3 hours, remove from the freezer and mix again. Do not overmix, as the cream can turn to butter.

After you've mixed the ice cream 4 times, cover the bowl tightly and return it to the freezer for at least 2 hours to freeze thoroughly. Eat immediately, as homemade ice cream is best when fresh.

HOW TO STORE IT Kept frozen and tightly covered, it will keep for at least a week, though you may need to blend again gently before serving.

PLUS: chocolate and vanilla (and other) ice creams

INSTRUCTIONS To make chocolate ice cream, omit the jam and zest and add 3 tablespoons Dutch-process cocoa powder, 1/4 teaspoon vanilla extract, and 1/2 cup water. Freeze and mix as above.

To make vanilla ice cream, make only half the syrup (using 1/2 cup water and 1/2 cup sugar), and infuse it with 3 scraped and chopped vanilla beans (see page 30), increase the milk to 3/4 cup, and add 1/2 teaspoon vanilla extract. (Omit the jam and zest.) Freeze and mix as above.

What, you want more? Feel free to substitute other flavors of jam for the strawberry. Additionally, some ideas for items to fold into ice cream include: lemon curd, Chocolate Hazelnut Spread (page 110), Cacao Nibs (page 78), ground toasted nuts, crumbled cookies and cake, chopped candy canes, shaved high-quality chocolate, and minced candied citrus peel (page 114). Also, feel free to replace the vanilla extract in either the chocolate or the vanilla ice cream with other flavored extracts, such as peppermint, orange, or almond.

ice cream cones

Makes 8 cones

TIME COMMITMENT
about 45 minutes

In truth, an ice cream cone is merely a large sugar cookie. The trick is in the shaping, and it will probably take you a few practice cones to get a leakproof cone into shape before the cookie hardens. That said, don't forget that a marshmallow is a great stop-gap plug for any cones that are not fully sealed on the bottom. Additionally, no one will judge you harshly if you ditch the cone shape altogether and make edible ice cream bowls instead. Seriously. Pair this with the homemade strawberry ice cream on page 140 and you are a rock star.

1/2 cup all-purpose flour

1 1/4 cups confectioners' sugar

1/2 teaspoon kosher salt

3 eggs

4 tablespoons vegetable oil, plus more for the pan

2 tablespoons milk

1 teaspoon vanilla extract, homemade (page 30) or store-bought

INSTRUCTIONS In a medium mixing bowl, whisk together the flour, sugar, and salt.

In a separate bowl, whisk the eggs until frothy. Stream in the oil, whisking as you go, then whisk in the milk.

Add the wet ingredients into the dry and whisk until smooth. Stir in the vanilla.

Set a small cup, a small spoon, and a champagne flute or other tall, thin glass near your work area. Heat a 10-inch skillet over medium heat (you will adjust the heat as necessary as you cook the cones).

Once the pan is hot, brush it with oil. Measure 3 tablespoons of the cone batter into a small cup. Lift the pan from the heat and pour the batter into the center of the pan, tilting the pan around in a circle as you pour. The idea is to spread a thin circular coating of batter evenly around the bottom of the pan. Do your best to get the batter into a circle as large as the pan's bottom.

Let this "crêpe" cook for about 2 minutes, until the edges are brown and the top side appears to be drying. Using a pancake turner, gently lift up the entire circular edge of the crêpe and flip it over, letting it cook for 1 to 2 minutes more, until brown. Note that it will not be an all-over brown, but will instead have a rather swirly pattern.

Remove the finished crêpe and transfer it to a work surface. As soon as it's cool enough to handle, after 20 to 25 seconds, work quickly to shape it into a cone. Fold up a half-inch edge on one side of the circle, creating a flat bottom. Then, bring one side up and over into a cone shape (narrow at the bottom, open at the top) and fold over the second side to follow suit. Quickly and gently, place your cone in the champagne flute so that the bottom of the cone can be sealed more tightly. Using a spoon inserted down into the center of the internal fold at the cone's bottom tip, press the seams into place to seal any gaps and to help

// CONTINUED

ice cream cones, CONTINUED

the cone hold its shape. Ideally, looking down in the bottom of the cone, you don't see any holes. (And if you do, inserting a marshmallow into the gap will help keep from dribbling ice cream on your shirt.)

Let the cone cool in the champagne flute as you make and shape the next cone, then remove it and lay it down on its side on a cooling rack. Make all 8 cones in this way.

Eat promptly, as the cones don't stay crispy for more than a couple of hours.

HOW TO STORE IT Store unwrapped on the countertop for up to 3 hours.

ice cream sandwiches

Makes eighteen 2 by 3-inch ice cream sandwiches

TIME COMMITMENT
about 4 hours

Anyone at any time can smash ice cream between two cookies and have a frozen treat at the ready. But I was going for something more like the soft cookie/thin layer of cake that is the culinary ideal of the classic rectangular wrapped ice cream sandwich. By the way, the "bread" of the ice cream sandwich, in my humble opinion, comes in only one flavor: chocolate.

1 cup all-purpose flour

2 cups sugar

$1/2$ cup Dutch-process cocoa powder

$1/2$ teaspoon kosher salt

2 eggs

$3/4$ cup vegetable oil

$3/4$ cup milk

2 teaspoons vanilla extract

1 quart ice cream, homemade (page 140) or store-bought

INSTRUCTIONS Preheat the oven to 350°F, with the rack in the center of the oven. Cut a piece of parchment paper large enough to cover the bottom of a large (17 by 12 by $3/4$-inch) rimmed baking sheet with a 2-inch or so handle of paper on either side. Press the paper into the edges of the pan.

In a large mixing bowl, whisk together the flour, sugar, cocoa, and salt. In a separate bowl, beat the eggs and pour the oil into it, whisking as you go. Pour the egg and oil mixture into the dry ingredients. Stir in the milk and then the vanilla, mixing until the batter is smooth.

Pour the batter into the prepared baking sheet and spread it evenly across the entire pan.

Bake the sandwich-making cake for about 13 minutes, or until it is dry all over and a toothpick inserted in the center comes out clean.

Let cool in the pan for 10 minutes, and then run a clean knife along the edges to make sure the cake isn't sticking. Invert the cake onto a cooling rack, peeling off the parchment, and let cool completely, about 45 minutes.

About 15 minutes before you're ready to make ice cream sandwiches, take the ice cream out of the freezer to soften.

Invert the cooled cake back into the pan. Using a sharp knife, cut the cake in half along the shorter side of the rectangle. Spread the softened ice cream (and yes, it's okay to mix flavors!) on one half of the cake. Using a spatula or bench scraper, carefully pick up the other half of the cake and place it over the ice cream, firmly pressing the top of the sandwich into place. Wrap that side of the baking sheet tightly in plastic wrap or foil and freeze for 2 hours or more.

If you're wrapping your ice cream sandwiches for later use, have torn pieces of aluminum foil ready to go (I like to score my giant ice cream sandwich into eighteen 2 by

// CONTINUED

3-inch sandwiches, so I tear off 18 short pieces of foil). With a wet, sharp knife, cut 3 equal-size segments, lengthwise, and then 6 pieces on the short side (you will need to keep wetting the knife periodically). If you are truly design-driven, feel free to trim away the uneven edges of the sandwiches as well. No one will notice if you eat the trimmings.

Working quickly, wrap 4 sandwiches at a time and move them back into the freezer. When all the sandwiches have been wrapped, transfer them to zip-top bags or airtight containers.

HOW TO STORE IT Kept frozen, these will for last up to 3 months.

index